Breaking Through

Building a World-Class Wealth Management Business

John J. Bowen Jr.,

Patricia J. Abram

and Jonathan Powell

This book is dedicated to all who made it possible:

Our corporate and coaching clients,
who taught us what truly works in our industry

Our teammates at CEG Worldwide,
who brought it all together

And our families,
who make it all worthwhile

Table of Contents

CHAPTER 1

Your Future Success

Your Future Success

What a fabulous industry we're in. As a financial advisor, you have opportunities before you that are greater today than ever before. In light of this extraordinary potential, we have written this book to provide you with a clear road map for achieving your greatest possible success and creating a business that's everything you've always hoped it would be.

Let's set some context. The United States, the world's wealthiest nation and the undisputed leader of free-market capitalism, has 301 million people and 108 million households. Of those households, 2.7 million have more than $1 million in investable assets.

Every major study that we have conducted here at CEG Worldwide, a leading industry coaching and consulting firm, shows that more than 90 percent of these affluent individuals want to work with a top financial advisor—if only they can find the right one. If that's the case, why are so many advisors not achieving everything they want? Why are so many stuck at the same income level, with the same business model and the same clients? Why aren't more advisors moving swiftly toward the success that they know can be theirs?

Finding the answers to these questions—and then sharing those answers with financial advisors— is the journey that the three authors of this book have been on their entire careers. Together, we have more than 80 years of industry experience, serving as financial advisors, corporate investment and insurance executives, and now as partners in CEG Worldwide.

We also have three other things of great value to share with you:

- An extraordinary depth of empirical research—real facts and figures—about how our industry is changing and about what works and what doesn't work
- Proven strategies for success—strategies that are replicable, reliable and road-tested by the hundreds of advisors who've been through our coaching programs

■ A commitment to sharing what we've learned so that you can achieve major breakthroughs and transform your practice into the business you've always wanted

What types of breakthroughs are we talking about? Consider the story below and the others found throughout this book of advisors who went through CEG Worldwide's coaching programs and, as a result, achieved levels of success that they'd previously only dreamed about.

Being Successful on Purpose: Doing What Works

There are approximately 765,000 registered financial advisors in the U.S. About 400,000 of them work with individuals. If these 400,000 advisors are chasing 2.7 million wealthy households—those with more than $1 million in investable assets—then simple math shows that there are fewer than seven such wealthy households per advisor. In fact, in our experience, most financial advisors are deeply unsatisfied with their incomes.

However, many of the advisors who've been through CEG Worldwide's coaching programs have been able to significantly grow their incomes as they transform their practices. Why are these advisors able to vault their productivity, build great businesses, do a great job for their clients and enjoy the quality of life that they want—while so many other advisors never seem to go anywhere? We wrote this book to answer these questions and to give you seven specific strategies that will jump-start you on your own path to success.

But before you start down that road, there's a simple philosophy

---

Real-World Success Story: Providing Wealth Management to the Right Niche

When advisor Scott Brown co-founded Wealth Management Group in 2001, he was content taking on just about any account he could get. But after meeting with three prospects worth $10 million, Brown and his partners realized they had a tremendous opportunity—and a big challenge. "We saw the potential to provide true wealth management to the affluent and make some serious money," he says. "The trouble was, we didn't know how to make it happen."

In the 12 months since joining CEG Worldwide's coaching program, Wealth Management Group has seen its assets under management nearly double, from $44 to $85 million, as Brown implemented various strategies and boosted his minimums from $100,000 to $1 million. Going forward, Brown expects his group to reach $500 million under management by 2010. "Our business today is completely different," he says. "Now we have the processes in place to be true wealth managers and differentiate ourselves in the marketplace." Brown also has something he didn't previously have: confidence. "I used to get nervous about saying the right things when meeting with big prospects, and I think it showed. Now I'm completely comfortable talking with the affluent, because I know we have a system that works."

Continued on following page

In particular, Brown credits two of the strategies highlighted in this book. The first is the Consultative Client Management Process, discussed in Chapter 4, a proven approach for working with clients to uncover and address their deepest financial concerns, values and needs. "The consultative process helps us get investors to really think about their goals, which in turn builds a deep level of trust and communication between us," Brown says. "People are blown away by the questions we've learned to ask them, and they can't wait to work with us."

Brown and his partners have also seen the value of focusing on the *right* wealthy niche, as discussed in Chapter 3. "I've learned to stop trying to be all things to all people and to work exclusively with the right types of affluent investors for me," Brown says. In his case, that means serving investors who are Family Stewards and concerned most about taking care of their families, including retirees and local farmers who have sold their properties and need help investing the proceeds. Brown has established himself in this niche by meeting with centers of influence in his target market, including attorneys and developers who work with these landowners. As a result, Brown says, "I'm becoming the first person they think of when their clients need help with managing their money."

All advisor success stories profile actual CEG Worldwide coaching program participants.

you must embrace: If you want to succeed, you must be successful *on purpose*. You are unlikely to haphazardly stumble into great success. Instead, you need a deliberate, focused approach to forging a highly profitable business that serves your clients well and provides you with the lifestyle you want.

Ironically, most advisors are already successful with the investment side of their businesses. Yes, we might debate the fine points of exactly how often to rebalance a portfolio or whether one should favor international over domestic funds at a particular point in time. However, so much academic research has been done on investment methodology and asset allocation that most advisors are doing a sound job with their clients' investments. We might argue about the last 5 percent of how to manage our clients' money, but 95 percent of the solution is clearly visible and available to any advisor willing to use it.

But when it comes to how advisors manage their practices, things are quite different. Most advisors approach their businesses in a kind of entrepreneurial fog, caught up in the day-to-day necessities of making a living and without a clear direction. Some firms provide advisors with ongoing training opportunities, but for the most part these are product-centric or technically oriented. Little thought is generally given to practice management and business development.

To fill this gap, CEG Worldwide has applied the rigors of empirical research used so successfully on the investment side to the best practices of top advisors. We've studied thousands of financial advisors and affluent clients and have identified the best practices

Your Future Success

of the leading advisors in the industry—those who consistently earn the top incomes. We've taken this knowledge and distilled it into seven key strategies. These strategies—which form the basis for our in-depth coaching program—have enabled many advisors to be successful on purpose and build the practices and lifestyles they've always wanted. Now we're sharing them with you.

An Overview of the Seven Strategies

Based on extensive industry research and our experience in working with hundreds of advisors in our coaching program and thousands of advisors throughout our combined careers, we've found that the most successful advisors regularly rely on seven key strategies. In fact, it would be fair to say that in nearly every business decision that they're making, these top advisors work toward mastering these seven strategies. Each of these strategies is further composed of a number of specific tactics, many of which we will discuss in detail in this book. As you read through the seven strategies, ask yourself how many of them you already follow. For those that you haven't already fully adopted, consider whether they make sense to you nonetheless on a gut level.

Strategy One: Attract Affluent Private Clients

In many ways life—and career success—is a numbers game. To succeed on purpose as an advisor, you simply *must* work with fewer, wealthier, clients. Leveraging our in-depth research and coaching experience, we'll first teach you what you need to know about the affluent. Then we'll show you how to focus your

Real-World Success Story: Comprehensive Coaching Really Works

CPA Ernest Clark, president of Jackson Thornton Asset Management in Dothan, Alabama, has seen his firm make great progress since he entered CEG Worldwide's coaching program. Assets under management have soared a whopping 100 percent—from $250 million to $500 million—in just over a year and a half. These days, Clark is starting to think it's time to boost that goal. "At one time, $1 billion sounded audacious, but now I think that we may have aimed too low."

Clark says the reason for these rapid results is a shift from building just a single aspect of his firm to generating success across the entire enterprise. "We were always working on getting clients, but we hadn't spent much time on business planning and strategic thinking. So we didn't need a tune-up in one area—we needed a comprehensive solution, and that's what the coaching program offers."

Clark began by quickly learning and implementing the consultative process for working with clients. "It allows us to get an extremely deep understanding of clients' needs and to serve those needs quicker. That's cut the time it takes to turn a prospect into a client, which in turn has led to faster referrals and stronger business growth."

Continued on following page

What's more, Clark has overcome a hurdle that had held him back for years: asking for referrals. "CPAs hate rejection, and that's why we were terrible at asking for referrals. The coaching program taught us how to position ourselves to ask for referrals effectively—and get them. Now we live off referrals."

business—and create a more desirable quality of life for yourself—by identifying and targeting a specific market niche. We'll share a wealth of tactics for attracting the affluent, such as interviewing centers of influence (COIs) in your niche and making use of pull marketing techniques. With fewer, wealthier clients you'll be able to establish intimate client relationships and deliver far better service. As a result, you'll be given more assets to manage and will generate referrals for additional wealthy clients in your target niche.

Strategy Two: Strengthen Client Relationships

It's sometimes said that people don't care how much you know until they know how much you care. By working very closely with your clients—by implementing the consultative client relationship management approach that we've developed and will spell out for you—you'll show them just how much you care. As you strengthen your client relationships, you'll build the foundation for a wealth management business that will be in alignment both with what your clients want and with what you can profitably provide while achieving the lifestyle you desire.

Strategy Three: Capture Assets and Acquire Clients

Since investments produce the lion's share of most advisors' revenue, we'll show you systematic methods both for generating an endless stream of prequalified prospects and for capturing more assets from existing clients. For example, we'll teach you how to capitalize on the fact that 84.6 percent of satisfied affluent clients would be happy to provide referrals. Also, since so many of the very best advisors owe a good deal of their success to referrals from other professional advisors, such as attorneys and accountants, we'll home in on exactly how to find and work with these other professionals. Often, it's not even a question of correctly positioning yourself, because the business is already there for the asking. Instead, you just have to know that it's there and how to ask for it. We'll show you how to do both.

Strategy Four: Manage Your Practice as a Business

Consider the great opportunity before you today: Our research shows that, on average, financial advisors delivering true wealth management earned net incomes of $881,000 in 2006. Now, you may not have thought that you were signing up to be an entrepreneur when you entered our industry. Nonetheless, we're going to explain why you owe it to all your stakeholders—including your clients—to build not just a good practice and a good job, but also a great and deftly managed business. One important difference between having a great business and having even a great job is whether the business is sustainable without you. We'll show you how to build a business that can hum along—even grow and expand—even when you're not there.

Strategy Five: Partner with Institutions and Other Professionals

By working well with others, you can accomplish far more than you can on your own. We'll show you how to work with the range of financial institutions and firms that want to partner with you—to their advantage, your advantage and your clients' advantage. In many cases both you and your clients will be better off in the long run if you turn to dedicated specialists to provide many types of investment-related services. We'll help you get clear about the tools you most need to best serve your clients, and then we'll show you how to seek out and work with those firms that are aligned with the kind and quality of services you want to provide. You'll end up with more time for client-facing activities and your clients will end up with better service.

**Real-World Success Story:
Invigorated Leadership Focused on the Affluent**

Tom Rabaut remembers his first thought upon entering CEG Worldwide's coaching program. "I said to myself, 'I manage less than $60 million in assets,'" says Rabaut, founder of The Fidelity Group in Troy, Michigan. "I'm small potatoes compared to the other guys in the room and I don't belong here."

But by the end of day one, Rabaut knew he was where he needed to be. "I almost instantly saw that I had been running my business the wrong way and that my management style was holding me back from creating a firm that was successful on purpose. The world literally changed for me that day."

Rabaut—the owner of a small four-advisor firm—stopped treating his firm as an enterprise consisting of multiple owners and instead began operating as a lifestyle boutique designed around a single principal. "In the past I never made decisions without consulting all of my employees. I wasn't the captain of my ship, and the result was that big strategic decisions never really got made or implemented. Now I am empowered to take this firm forward and deliberately make big improvements."

Continued on following page

Intriguingly, Rabaut's staff is now more on board with his approach than ever before, despite being involved less in the decision-making process. "One of my most loyal employees said to me, 'You're finally seeing everything through and really leading us.'"

Just as impressive is where that leadership has already taken the firm. Rabaut discovered two underserved groups of affluent individuals in his area: retiring university professors and health care administrators about to receive large sums from their retirement packages. Armed with that knowledge, he set out to aggressively target that select market opportunity. "We used to work primarily with middle-income clients because it seemed so difficult to go after the affluent, and we'd take pretty much anyone who was breathing," Rabaut says. "Now I'm focusing exclusively on building a wealth management firm that caters specifically to those groups."

To that end, Rabaut has begun reducing his client base (he expects to go from 290 clients to roughly 150 ideal target clients) and increasing his minimum account size from $50,000 to $500,000 to support the firm's new focused business model. In addition, he's meeting with key local niche leaders to learn about their crucial issues and needs—information he's using to develop a marketing strategy that will pull ideal clients to his doorstep. "I've learned that working with a small group of the right clients and charging them premium prices is the way to win."

Strategy Six: Commit to Lifelong Learning

The biggest asset any of us has is our human capital. We describe how to nurture your own human capital and the human capital of the members of your team. Your reward will be renewed ideas, rekindled enthusiasm and enhanced skill sets. Sometimes those of us who achieve a modicum of success stop attending both personal and industry-relevant workshops and conferences because we feel these are designed for those who are less successful. In truth, as you become more successful it is even *more* important to be thoughtful about maximizing your human capital in order to continue becoming all that you are capable of being.

Strategy Seven: Realize Maximum Equity

Whether you are an equity stakeholder in your business or an intrapreneur—an employee in an independent firm or in a wirehouse—we'll show you how to work toward maximizing your business's value. We'll share with you some of the secrets to consistently making smart decisions that will dramatically increase the value of your business. Far too often our businesses become cluttered with nonessential items and processes. But to create maximum value, we'll show you how to build a business that runs effortlessly, one that makes your competitors scratch their heads and wonder how you make it all seem so simple. Even if you're never going to sell your business, in the long run each and every one of us will transfer our accounts to others, and therefore it pays to always run your business "as if" you are planning to sell it for the greatest possible price.

How to Use This Book

As you read through the seven strategies, begin to think of what might be possible if you deployed these strategies. Begin to imagine the ideal business that you might have—the one that gives you the financial success, the benefits for your clients and the personal lifestyle you've always wanted. Don't get caught up in individual strategies or tactics. Instead, give yourself permission to dream big—as big as you can—about your ideal business. Let that dream grow while you read this book. We promise you that the opportunity is out there for you to become as successful as you want. We will show you how to turn that opportunity into reality.

As for how to make all this real, we'll discuss that generally throughout the book but specifically in the next chapter and Chapter 10. And at the end of the book, we'll tell you about a Web site where you'll find an interactive assessment tool. After answering a series of questions, this tool will help you identify the gaps in your practice and some of the actions that you might want to take. But for now, we invite you to sit back and relax, open your mind and consider something that we all face: the knowing-doing gap.

CHAPTER 2

Bridging the Knowing-Doing Gap

Bridging the Knowing-Doing Gap

*Many of us believe we have tremendous untapped potential. We yearn to squeeze all the juice out of our lives and careers but don't know how. Even when we do know how (or **think** we do), we somehow end up not doing anything about it anyway.*

There are two pieces of good news here.

First: You're not alone. Many people, including many successful financial advisors, are frustrated by their inability to move to a higher level of success, even if they think they know what they should do next. But knowing what you need to do and actually doing it are two very different things. We call this distinction the "knowing-doing gap."

Second: This chapter will explain exactly how to close the knowing-doing gap. Of course, *knowing* how to do this and actually *doing* it are two very different things. As Yogi Berra said, "In theory there is no difference between theory and practice. In practice there is."

The Map Is Not the Territory

Where does the knowing-doing gap come from? Consider how we are educated in our culture. For the most part, teachers put forward facts and theories that we study and memorize, and we repeat these back during tests. If we pass these tests—especially if we ace them—we think that we really "know" the subject matter and feel pretty good about ourselves.

However, such conceptual learning doesn't give us a very good sense of how to actually *do* things. For example, you might take a seminar or read some books on turning your practice into a great business. But concept-oriented books and seminars can at best expand and reorient our thinking, and very few people can move directly from better thinking into successful action.

If you've ever been involved in building or remodeling a home or office, you know that there can be a big difference between your conception of the project's outcome and what happens as it is actually built. We think conceptually, but we have to act in the real world, and the real world often doesn't match up with our concepts. As Alfred Korzybski famously said, "The map is not the territory."

This distinction holds for nearly everything you do. For example, you may have an abstract idea of how your first meeting with a client will go, but when you sit down with this particular person, things end up going quite differently. The same thing can hold true as you embark upon building a world-class wealth management practice. Even if you know precisely what your goal is and think you know exactly how to get there, things often work out differently than planned. Like a construction project, things often go wrong, take longer or turn out another way. If you accept this likelihood up front, you are much more likely to hold steadfast to your plan and succeed in the long run.

Minding the Gaps

Before turning to exactly how to step over the knowing-doing gap, it's important to understand that there are a number of levels within the gap that can impede your progress, as shown in **Exhibit 2.1**.

EXHIBIT 2.1		Levels of the Knowing-Doing Gap	
Level	**Type of Gap**	**Advisor Status**	**Gap Analysis**
4	No gap	Advisor is on his or her way to creating a great business.	All levels of the knowing-doing gap have been successfully overcome.
3	Knowing-doing gap	Advisor starts doing what needs to be done but gets stuck or gives up along the way.	This is the knowing-doing gap proper; it can be overcome by strong commitment and the ability to coordinate consistent actions with long-term vision.
2	Commitment gap	Advisor knows what needs to be done but doesn't begin doing it.	There is a lack of motivation, courage or commitment.
1	Knowledge gap	Advisor wants to change but doesn't know how to go forward or has outdated or inaccurate information.	There is a lack of empirical knowledge about what really works and what needs to be done.
0	No awareness of gaps	Advisor is satisfied with status quo.	With no desire to change, there is no awareness of any gaps.

Source: CEG Worldwide.

Advisors at Level 0 are satisfied with things the way things are. Not knowing or caring about Paris, they are content to stay on the farm. As a result, they don't contemplate any major changes or new actions. (If you've read this far, then you're beyond this level.)

At Level 1, advisors know that much more is possible and are frustrated with their current business-es. They may be good or even exceptional at investing and managing clients' wealth but don't have the entrepreneurial perspective or practice management expertise necessary to move forward. That's where this book and our more in-depth coaching programs become invaluable.

At Level 2, an advisor knows what needs to be done but doesn't wholeheartedly step into crafting the necessary plans and taking the required actions. This may be due to a lack of motivation or clarity or a general unwillingness to commit to being successful on purpose. Often, advisors at this level let the unimportant urgent daily grind get in the way of implementing necessary changes. It's critical that these advisors step over this gap by fully committing themselves to making the needed plans and act-ing in accordance with those plans. At the end of this chapter we'll say more about the rewards that follow from having courage and taking action.

At Level 3, advisors are fully committed to being successful on purpose. Still, because many things can go wrong or at least differently than planned, many advisors get stuck or give up short of creating the business that they dream of. This is the knowing-doing gap proper and can be overcome with the integral approach to both knowing and doing that we describe next.

Persistent, courageous advisors can overcome this final knowing-doing gap to reach Level 4 and cre-ate the profitable world-class businesses and lifestyles they have always dreamed of.

Coordinating Consistent Action and Long-Term Vision

Suppose you read this book, are committed to changing and understand what you need to do to build a great business. Now the hard part begins: stepping out into the real world—the one beyond your conceptual maps—and making it happen. You must convert your knowledge into real-world actions that result in the business you want. Obviously, making all this happen is very different from just talk-ing or thinking about it.

What typically will happen next is that you begin bumping into lots of unexpected barriers. Managers, partners, employees, clients, regulators, and broker-dealers or custodians: No one will behave quite as you expected. Soon enough, you begin thinking, "All that vision stuff is a lot of baloney"—especially when you have to deal with your in-laws, income taxes, office politics and paying the bills. Before long, you are back to reacting to the world as it actually is, and the "knowing" element of your vision is lost.

Combining knowing and doing—putting action and vision together—is a huge challenge for almost everyone. With all the pressures we face, it's very difficult to consistently act in service of our long-term goals. It's almost as if there were a current pushing us away from what we want to achieve.

It will help you stay on course to recognize that there are two domains of knowing and two domains of doing. The result is the four-quadrant Integral Knowing-Doing Grid, as shown in **Exhibit 2.2.**

EXHIBIT 2.2	The Integral Knowing-Doing Grid	
	Internal *What you know*	**External** *What you do*
Individual *Domain of the person*	*Me*: individual concerns, thoughts, meanings, values and identity *Field*: depth psychology	*It*: individual actions and results; how the individual works *Field*: behaviorism
Group *Domain of the group*	*We*: shared concerns, thoughts, meanings, values, group membership *Field*: anthropology	*Its*: systems, group actions and results, rules and procedures; what firms do *Field*: systems research

Source: Ken Wilber, *A Brief History of Everything*, 1996.

The upper-right quadrant is individual action—what you actually do. The upper-left quadrant represents your personal beliefs and thoughts, including who you are as an advisor, the quality of service you want to provide to your clients and what you want to make of yourself and your business.

The lower-left quadrant is the social sphere. It represents the conversations you have with other industry members and others who influence how you think and help you develop. This includes coaches, your peers, and others in your work and personal life who help you to enlarge your thinking. Finally, the lower-right quadrant represents the systems you put into place that enable you to move forward, make things happen and bring your vision into being.

Most of us end up working in just one or two of these quadrants. For example, some of us just take individual actions. We act, act, act, perhaps calling clients, making presentations or selling products. But in all this acting, we end up not learning much about ourselves, we fail to put systems into place and we tend to repeat our mistakes. Likewise, others of us are very good at working on our personal identity, self-image and vision for our futures. We may be really good at writing out our vision statements, but our visions never seem to happen.

To overcome the knowing-doing gap—to get from Level 3 to Level 4—you must tap into each of the quadrants on a regular basis. Find ways to link them up and move from one to another so that they reinforce each other.

For instance, suppose that, as a result of reading this book, you decide to be much more selective about the new clients you take on in the future. You determine the specific market niche you can serve best and most profitably and commit to working only with clients from this niche. This is an action in the external world and so resides in the upper-right quadrant.

To link this with the other quadrants, ask yourself what you are learning from this action and how you feel about it. Then have a conversation about it with one of your colleagues, coaches or loved ones. See how you can incorporate what you learn in this conversation back into your actions as you move forward. Then take another action in the real world. See how that has improved your self-knowledge, next talk to your colleagues about it and then use their feedback to put together an even better system.

Linking the quadrants like this—spiraling out from what you actually do and know to what others think and advise to systems that help you lock it all into place—not only keeps you learning over time, but actually helps you to achieve your vision by encouraging you to take more action and create ever-better systems. You will find it much easier to continue to forge forward when your conceptual plans come up against real-world obstacles. Even in the face of temporary "failures" (perhaps better thought of as "accelerated learning opportunities"), you'll be able to continue to coordinate your actions with your long-term vision. And voilá! You'll find yourself on the other side of the knowing-doing gap—well on your way to the business of your dreams.

Frustration into Courage, Action into Rewards

We've often found that elite advisors—those who succeed in transforming their businesses—are individuals who start out somewhat frustrated. Although their peers and clients see them as successful, they are nonetheless frustrated because they want to create truly great businesses that produce substantially greater incomes, afford a more desirable lifestyle and provide better client service.

So it's okay to be frustrated. It means you are aware that you are missing an opportunity to be and do more. By recognizing and then harnessing that frustration, you will be far more likely to overcome the knowing-doing gap and successfully execute on the strategies we describe in this book. We will lay out your road map to success, but it will be up to you to start moving toward your destination.

As we saw earlier, it's easier to learn something conceptually than it is to actually do it. Taking action requires courage, steadfastness and a willingness to fail, as well as the intelligence to learn from our mistakes.

We all know what it's like to try something new and fall flat on our faces in front of an important client, management or our peers. Most of the time we avoid such possibilities at all costs. But the most successful people are willing to try new things and fail many times until they get it right. It's like learning to ice skate: If you don't fall down at first, you're not trying hard enough.

It boils down to this: No amount of conceptual learning can take the place of real-world action and feedback. We can provide you with powerful strategies and tactics, but we can't provide you with the courage to act. (For some advisors, having someone along on the journey makes it a great deal easier to take action. For these advisors, enrolling in a coaching program may make a great deal of sense, as we'll discuss in Chapter 8.)

Obviously, if you don't act, you won't get the rewards that come from taking action. And if you don't take action—if this ends up being just one more business book that you read and put away on your shelf—you're unlikely to achieve the transformative changes you desire. So dig deep and find the courage to act to implement the seven strategies we will turn to next.

Ultimately, the greatest rewards come to those advisors who:

- Have the wisdom to seek out knowledge and guidance about what works
- Have the courage to take action despite the possibility of failure
- Are willing to accept and learn from the heat of real-world feedback
- Consistently coordinate both knowing and doing with long-term vision

If you can do these four things—and with our help we believe you can—the business of your dreams can become your everyday reality far sooner than you think.

CHAPTER 3

Attract Affluent Clients

Attract Affluent Clients

Financial advisors are often taught from day one to seek out as many clients as they can and sell them as much product as possible. Unfortunately, this is rarely highly profitable. Advisors who follow this approach all too often end up with lackluster practices and unfulfilled career dreams.

We recommend a different path: working with fewer but wealthier clients. But who are these clients and what do they want from their advisors? How can you attract them so that you can build a more successful business and create a better lifestyle for yourself while effectively meeting their financial challenges?

A clear understanding of the affluent will be the foundation of your success. You'll be able to identify your optimum target market niche—the affluent clients whom you can serve best and most profitably—and then to systematically position yourself to attract these clients. And by knowing exactly what the affluent want, you can implement the business model that will meet their most important financial needs.

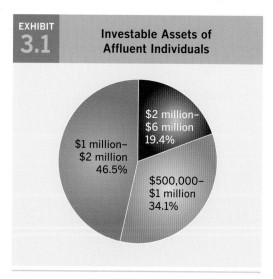

EXHIBIT 3.1

Investable Assets of Affluent Individuals

$2 million–$6 million 19.4%

$1 million–$2 million 46.5%

$500,000–$1 million 34.1%

N = 1,417 affluent individuals.
Source: Russ Alan Prince and David A. Geracioti, *Cultivating the Middle-Class Millionaire*, 2005.

The Affluent: A Demographic Profile

In 2005, industry researcher Russ Alan Prince headed up a survey of 1,417 individuals with between $500,000 and $5 million in liquid assets and net worths between $1 million and $10 million.

As **Exhibit 3.1** shows, nearly two-thirds of those surveyed (65.9 percent) have more than $1 million in investable assets. Take a step back, let this number sink in and stop worrying about there not being *enough* affluent individuals for you to work with. Start thinking bigger and better (clients), and soon your business will be bigger and better as well.

Now, to really understand and best serve affluent clients, it will be their total assets, not just investable assets, that you'll be interested in. A look at net worth, as shown in **Exhibit 3.2**, reinforces the positive picture about the level of affluence in the United States. Just over half (53.9 percent) of the survey group have net worths between $1 and $3 million, while 46.1 percent have net worths between $3 million and $10 million.

Surprisingly, very few affluent individuals actually think of themselves as being wealthy but instead view themselves as being middle- or upper-middle class. In fact, as **Exhibit 3.3** shows, *none* of those surveyed classified themselves as being wealthy, and 42.6 percent thought they were just middle-class. As you begin to attract and work with affluent clients, remember that unless they are in the ultra-high-net-worth range, with a net worth of perhaps $25 million or higher, they are likely to solidly identify with the values, concerns and dreams of the middle class.

What about the ages of the affluent? It's generally difficult to accumulate wealth when one is young, so it's not surprising, as **Exhibit 3.4** shows, that only 31.0 percent of those surveyed were under 55. As for gender, 67.8 percent of those surveyed were male.

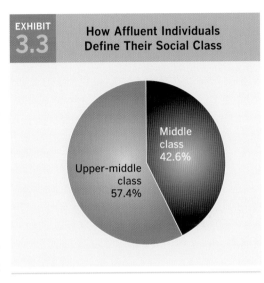

EXHIBIT 3.3
How Affluent Individuals Define Their Social Class

N = 1,417 affluent individuals.
Source: Russ Alan Prince and David A. Geracioti, *Cultivating the Middle-Class Millionaire*, 2005.

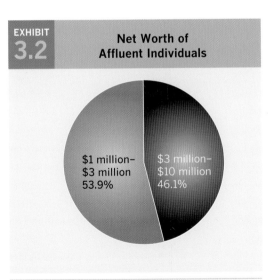

EXHIBIT 3.2
Net Worth of Affluent Individuals

N = 1,417 affluent individuals.
Source: Russ Alan Prince and David A. Geracioti, *Cultivating the Middle-Class Millionaire*, 2005.

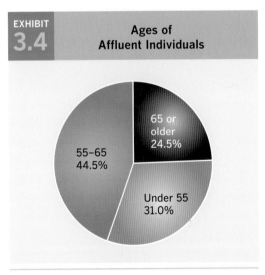

EXHIBIT 3.4
Ages of Affluent Individuals

N = 1,417 affluent individuals.
Source: Russ Alan Prince and David A. Geracioti, *Cultivating the Middle-Class Millionaire*, 2005.

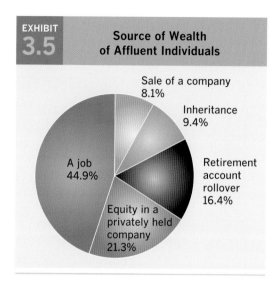

EXHIBIT 3.5

Source of Wealth of Affluent Individuals

Sale of a company 8.1%

Inheritance 9.4%

A job 44.9%

Retirement account rollover 16.4%

Equity in a privately held company 21.3%

N = 1,417 affluent individuals.
Source: Russ Alan Prince and David A. Geracioti, *Cultivating the Middle-Class Millionaire*, 2005.

Next, although many of us assume that a great number of wealthy people have inherited their wealth, **Exhibit 3.5** shows that only 9.4 percent of those surveyed did so. Instead, the great majority made their wealth the old-fashioned way, through a job or through some kind of ongoing business endeavor.

Nine High-Net-Worth Personalities

Many advisors tend to treat all affluent clients the same, but this is a mistake. If you've ever taken a personality profile test, such as the Myers-Briggs, you'll recognize the value of methodically classifying individuals according to different psychological types. Research from Russ Alan Prince on the psychographic characteristics of the affluent, which includes a psychological framework that parses wealthy individuals into nine high-net-worth psychological types, is useful for understanding the often subtle differences between affluent individuals. Our real-world experience confirms that while everyone has characteristics of more than one high-net-worth personality, virtually every individual has a dominant personality type along these lines.

This psychological framework applies to every aspect of attracting and serving affluent clients. It will also give you a window into many "why" questions: Why do the affluent choose the financial advisors they do, and why do they switch advisors? Why do some have many advisors, and others only one? Why do the affluent prefer certain services to others?

EXHIBIT 3.6

Distribution of the High-Net-Worth Personalities

Innovators 4.1%

Gamblers 5.0%

Accumulators 6.1%

VIPs 6.6%

Moguls 7.6%

The Anonymous 8.3%

Family Stewards 34.1%

Independents 16.8%

Phobics 11.4%

N = 1,417 affluent individuals.
Source: Russ Alan Prince and David A. Geracioti, *Cultivating the Middle-Class Millionaire*, 2005.

Exhibit 3.6 shows the distribution of the high-net-worth personality types, and Exhibit 3.7 gives a summary overview of each type. Two things are particularly worth noting. First, more than one-third of affluent individuals can be classified as Family Stewards, whose name alone immediately reveals some of what is most important to them. Second, while the three types that are most interested in investing per se—the Accumulators, Gamblers and Innovators—together constitute only 15.5 percent of the affluent, these prospective clients not only most frequently show up at public workshops and respond to direct mail, they also tend to be the most demanding and time-consuming of all clients. Caveat advisor!

EXHIBIT 3.7	The Nine High-Net-Worth Personalities

Family Stewards
- Dominant focus is to take care of their families.
- Conservative in personal and professional life.
- Not very knowledgeable about investing.

Independents
- Seek the personal freedom money makes possible.
- Feel investing is a necessary means to an end.
- Not interested in the process of investing or wealth management.

Phobics
- Are confused and frustrated by the responsibility of wealth.
- Dislike managing finances and avoid technical discussion of it.
- Choose advisors based on level of personal trust they feel.

The Anonymous
- Confidentiality is their prominent concern.
- Prize privacy for their financial affairs.
- Likely to concentrate assets with an advisor who protects them.

Moguls
- Control is a primary concern.
- Investing is another way of extending personal power.
- Decisive in decisions; rarely look back.

VIPs
- Investing results in ability to purchase status possessions.
- Prestige is important.
- Like to affiliate with institutions and advisors with leading reputations.

Accumulators
- Focused on making their portfolios bigger.
- Investments are performance-oriented.
- Tend to live below their means and spend frugally.

Gamblers
- Enjoy investing for the excitement of it.
- Tend to be very knowledgeable and involved.
- Exhibit a high risk tolerance.

Innovators
- Focused on leading-edge products and services.
- Sophisticated investors who like complex products.
- Tend to be technically savvy and highly educated.

Source: Russ Alan Prince and Brett Van Bortel, *The Millionaire's Advisor*™, 2003.

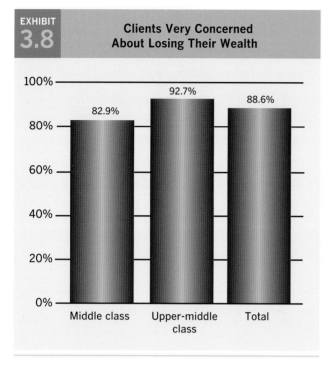

EXHIBIT 3.8

Clients Very Concerned About Losing Their Wealth

N = 1,417 affluent individuals.
Source: Russ Alan Prince and David A. Geracioti, *Cultivating the Middle-Class Millionaire*, 2005.

Key Concerns of the Affluent

The better we understand the key concerns of affluent clients and prospects, the better we can deliver an experience that exceeds their expectations. To begin with, although many financial advisors think their job is to *create* wealth, **Exhibit 3.8** clearly shows that the great majority of affluent clients are quite concerned about *losing* their wealth. But additional research shows that just 15.4 percent of 512 advisors surveyed believe that 20 percent or more of their affluent clients are very concerned about losing their wealth. And interestingly, individuals who identified themselves as upper-middle class felt even more strongly about this issue: The higher their perceived social class, the more concerned they are with holding on to their wealth. As an advisor to the affluent, then, your first commandment is to assist clients in *preserving their wealth*.

EXHIBIT 3.9

Clients' Concerns About Tax Mitigation			
	Net Worth		
Tax Concern	**$1 million– $3 million**	**$3 million– $10 million**	**Total**
Mitigating income taxes	90.1%	77.3%	84.7%
Mitigating estate taxes	21.7%	81.3%	49.2%
Mitigating capital gains taxes	27.1%	58.5%	41.7%

N = 1,417 affluent individuals.
Source: Russ Alan Prince and David A. Geracioti, *Cultivating the Middle-Class Millionaire*, 2005.

Another key issue is tax mitigation. As **Exhibit 3.9** shows, mitigating income taxes is a concern of more than 90 percent of those with net worths between $1 million and $3 million and of more than three-quarters of those with net worths between $3 million and $10 million. For those in the higher net-worth range, mitigating estate and capital gains taxes are also major concerns.

Of course the affluent have many other concerns, as **Exhibit 3.10** shows. These range from ensuring that heirs, parents, children and grandchildren are taken care of to having adequate medical insurance, legal protection, personal security and retirement funding. Note that there are some significant (and sometimes counter-intuitive) differences between the two different net-worth categories.

EXHIBIT 3.10	Clients' Concerns About Personal Interests and Responsibilities		
	Net Worth		
Interest or Responsibility	**$1 million– $3 million**	**$3 million– $10 million**	**Total**
Ensuring that heirs are taken care of	66.9%	93.6%	79.2%
Having adequate medical insurance	78.1%	76.4%	77.3%
Having enough money in retirement	87.3%	53.0%	71.5%
Paying for children's or grandchildren's education	65.2%	28.6%	48.3%
Being sued	37.4%	58.8%	47.3%
Losing job or business	48.4%	30.5%	40.0%
Having high-quality personal security	17.8%	40.4%	28.2%
Taking care of parents	38.4%	16.1%	28.1%
Making meaningful gifts to charity	21.9%	34.8%	27.8%

N = 1,417 affluent individuals.
Source: Russ Alan Prince and David A. Geracioti, *Cultivating the Middle-Class Millionaire*, 2005.

With this table in mind, you can systematically design your client service in order to consistently address clients' concerns. In Chapter 4 we'll describe the consultative process that advisors in our coaching programs have found extremely effective not only in addressing the concerns of their affluent clients, but in capturing many billions of dollars in assets under management.

Importantly, additional research conducted by CEG Worldwide shows that there is a consistent disconnect between client concerns and advisors' perceptions of client concerns. This holds true whether the topic is wealth preservation, tax mitigation or the concerns listed in **Exhibit 3.10.**

Exhibit 3.11 highlights one very important disconnect between clients and advisors. Regardless of their level of investable assets, more than 70 percent of surveyed affluent individuals are concerned about working with a high-quality investment advisor, while on average just 11.9 percent of those surveyed are concerned with diversifying their investment portfolios. By contrast, another study found that 33.4 percent of 512 surveyed advisors believe that diversifying their investment portfolios is very important to their affluent clients.

So even though diversifying an investment portfolio and creating a proper asset allocation is today universally recognized as the hallmark of competent investment management, it's simply not as important to clients and potential clients as the perceived quality and expertise of their financial

EXHIBIT 3.11	Clients' Investment Management Concerns			
	Investable Assets			
Concern	**$500,000–$1 million**	**$1 million–$2 million**	**$2 million–$6 million**	**Total**
Working with a high-quality investment advisor	70.4%	73.7%	74.2%	72.7%
Diversifying investment portfolios	18.2%	11.2%	2.5%	11.9%

N = 1,417 affluent individuals.
Source: Russ Alan Prince and David A. Geracioti, *Cultivating the Middle-Class Millionaire*, 2005.

advisors. To grow a great business serving delighted affluent clients, the business model you design and the client experiences you deliver must start with where the client is, not with where we are or where we *think* the client is.

Identify Your Target Market Niche

With a clear idea of who the affluent are, it's time for you to make a critical decision: Exactly which types of affluent clients do you want to work with? Both you and your clients will be better off if you choose to work with fewer, wealthier clients. All of you will enjoy a wide variety of benefits when you pare down your clientele to a specific market niche.

Your clients will be better-served because you will have the depth of expertise required to recognize and either directly offer or otherwise find solutions for their specific needs and challenges. You will be better-off because you will need to put together just one set of adaptable solutions, services and strategic partners, freeing up your time to further focus on client relationships. And as you become known within your niche as *the* expert best able to meet the specific needs of your community, you are more likely to receive strong referrals. In short, when you specialize in a niche market, it's easier to become the expert your clients need and to position yourself as the expert your clients want, and it's easier and more cost-effective to provide world-class service that directly addresses all of your clients' needs.

A practice devoted to a specific client niche is almost always also a more enjoyable practice. When you work with one type of client whom you've consciously chosen, and whom you truly have an affinity for, you will likely be happier both on and off the job and much less likely to get "burned out." Your quality of life as an advisor will rise dramatically because you will be working with people you like, are interested in and have an affinity for.

If you think of a "niche" as a defined market that is particularly well-suited to your talents, skills and interests, then, as **Exhibit 3.12** suggests, there are a mind-boggling number of potential niches. Choose a niche that you are passionate about and don't be afraid to pioneer a brand new niche.

EXHIBIT 3.12	**Affluent Segments, with Specific Niche Examples**

Affluent Segment	Examples of Specific Niches Within Segment
Self-employed professionals	Radiologists, consultants, M&A attorneys
Independent salespeople	Financial product wholesalers, Gulfstream jet aircraft salespeople, medical device salespeople
Key corporate executives	Google, Exxon or AT&T senior executives
Artists and entertainers	Behind-the-camera television talent, screenplay writers, best-selling novelists
Professional athletes	Retired San Francisco 49ers stars, Atlanta Flames hockey players
Successful business builders	Local developers of high-end homes, 20-store McDonald's franchise owners
Prudent retirees (with $1 million or more in retirement funds)	Hewlett-Packard retirees, Lockheed Martin retirees, Chevron retirees
Widows	Widows with large estates working with the top local estate planning attorneys
Divorcees	Divorcees with large settlements working with the top local divorce planning attorneys
Inheritors	High-end estate planning attorneys in local market, local support groups for sudden wealth

Source: CEG Worldwide.

The trick is to relentlessly drill down to find the market niche that bests suits your skills and personality. Whom, in the best possible of all worlds, would you like to work with most? To whom could you provide so much value that it becomes easy to build the wealth management business of your dreams?

Once you've answered these questions, do some research to determine whether a particular niche really makes sense for you. We recommend this four-step process:

1. Identify several concentrations or sources of wealth in your geographic area.

2. Identify a few potential niche markets where you can add value and are likely to enjoy working with clients.

3. Interview centers of influence (COIs)—movers and shakers in the niche—as well as any niche members among your existing client base to identify significant potential opportunities.

4. Analyze your opportunities, choose a single primary niche and make it so!

The first step is the easiest. There are concentrations of wealth everywhere. Open your eyes, ears and mind to what's around you. (If you live in the middle of Iowa, your inquiry may need to embrace a larger geographic area than if you live in Manhattan.) If you live in Charlotte, North Carolina, consider executives from banking and related industries. If you live in Ann Arbor, Michigan, consider college professors, startup scientists or university administrators. If you live in Fort Lauderdale, Florida, consider retirees, widows and yacht owners.

Once you've laid out some broad possibilities, identify one or more niches in which you believe you can add substantial value and would enjoy working. If you enjoy your clients, the odds that you'll be energized by your work (and even more important, you will have fun while doing it) go up dramatically. Later we will discuss the number of contacts highly satisfied affluent clients have with their primary financial advisors and what those contacts

Identifying and Interviewing Centers of Influence

The most effective way to determine a niche's size and depth, how to best market to those in the niche, and the unique needs and challenges of its members is to interview centers of influence—the niche's movers and shakers. COIs are highly visible and influential individuals who have in-depth niche knowledge and are typically either niche members themselves or otherwise professionally related to the niche. Be creative when seeking out COIs, as there are trade organizations, consultants and affinity groups for nearly every conceivable area of interest. Look for key individuals such as these:

- Trade association executives and affinity group leaders
- Trade press publishers, editors and reporters
- Lawyers, accountants, consultants and other professionals specializing in the niche
- Leaders and esteemed niche members

Once you've determined an initial list of three to five COIs, the hardest part for most advisors is picking up the phone and requesting a meeting. Simply explain to the COI that you are a financial advisor doing research on a specific niche and that his or her name has come up as someone who is both knowledgeable and influential. State that you'd like to discuss over lunch the unique needs of those in the niche, and then suggest a convenient date, time and place. Almost no one will say no to a request that is both earnest and flattering, and for the price of

Continued on following page

a meal you'll get focused, in-depth market research.

Prepare for the interview by carefully constructing a set of specific but open-ended questions that build on what you already know about the niche. Cover the following areas:

- The primary challenges faced by niche members
- The size of the niche and the approximate average wealth of niche members
- The best ways to market to niche members
- Other professionals who specialize in offering services to the niche
- The trade, social, community and affinity groups and organizations that members of the niche and their spouses belong to
- Who your competitors in the niche are, along with their value propositions
- Industry events and publications of interest to niche members
- The identity of other niche COIs and other professional advisors to niche members (attorneys, accountants, etc.)

Close every COI interview with two final questions: "If you were me, knowing what you now know, what else should I have asked you?" and "May I give you a call if any additional questions come up?" Follow up after the meeting with a handwritten thank-you note. If the interview results in any specific successes, send another note or give the COI a call to keep him or her in the loop.

entail. For now, understand that you will need to talk about much more than just their investments, so look for niches where affluent individuals and you are likely to have interests in common.

Next, talk to the centers of influence in the niche or niches you are considering. COIs are the people around whom members of the niche naturally congregate. Your objective will be to build a community around these individuals, so you need to choose a niche in which you will be able to reach many prospective affluent clients where they work, play or otherwise get together. Interviewing COIs will help you accurately determine the viability of the niche and whether your initial understanding of the niche matches up to reality. (The sidebar beginning on the previous page provides detail on conducting effective COI interviews.)

If any of your existing clients are members of the niche, ask them for their perspectives on the niche generally and specifically how they feel that an advisor could better serve those in that niche. Also ask for introductions to others in the niche, especially COIs.

The final step is to evaluate all the information you've gathered and choose the best niche: one that offers significant opportunities yet is narrow enough for you to focus on effectively. While a few advisors "fall into" superb niches by accident, it generally takes a lot of hard work to determine the right niche and commit to making it your own.

Narrow It Down Once More: Define Your Ideal Client Profile

Once you've defined the niche on which you'll focus, create yet another filter for the clients with whom you'll work. Define an ideal client profile, a detailed description of the clients within your niche with whom you want to work. It should include the following information:

- **A general description of your ideal client.** Include stage of life (working vs. retired), industry, occupation, specific company and job (if appropriate), marital status, education level, age range and any other relevant demographic characteristics.

- **The geographic location of your ideal clients.** Don't spread yourself too thin.

- **Amount of investable assets.** Don't shoot too low here! Advisors often don't realize how easily they can move upmarket if they are willing to set the bar high. One useful guideline is the "Rule of Five." Take the top 20 percent of your clients, calculate their average investable assets and then multiply that figure by five.

- **Minimum assets under management and minimum fee.** Our research consistently shows that advisors who set higher investment minimums and have minimum fees have higher incomes.

- **Financial challenges.** What financial challenges are you most interested in helping solve? Be specific here.

- **Source of acquisition.** How do you want your ideal client to

---

Real-World Success Story: Interviewing Centers of Influence

When advisor Mike Hull began the coaching program, his ongoing struggle to understand the affluent market and build a strategic plan for his business ended—on day one. "I nearly fell off my chair during the first meeting, because I immediately saw what the affluent valued from an advisor," says Hull, president of Donaldson Capital Management in Evansville, Indiana. "I'd been searching for that information for months with no luck."

Since then, Hull has begun using CEG Worldwide's proprietary research on the affluent and key coaching program tactics to provide the highest level of service to the right clients as he seeks to grow assets under management from $280 million to $500 million during the next two years. Case in point: Hull's new focus on serving an ideal niche market he identified through the program—executives and retirees of Bristol-Myers Squibb. A former employee of the pharmaceutical giant, Hull has leveraged existing contacts as well as delivered a retirement seminar at the firm that helped him garner four new ideal clients last quarter—one of whom told Hull that "when people at Bristol talk retirement, they talk about you."

Continued on following page

To further strengthen the firm's credibility among that target niche, Hull and his associates have also met with more than 20 centers of influence—such as lawyers, accountants and affluent retirees—to fully understand the niche's key issues. "By following the coaching program's techniques, we've learned what affluent retirees are most worried about, and we're using that knowledge to demonstrate our ability to give them what they need most," says Hull.

come to you? Referrals? Strategic alliances? Seminars? Credibility marketing?

- **High-net-worth personality, compatibility and profitability.** Which of the high-net-worth personality types are you likely to work best with? Whom should you avoid?
- **Personal enjoyment and affinity.** What kind of affluent clients will you most enjoy working with? With whom do you share the most interests and avocations?

Summarize your ideal client profile on a single page. And while you're at it, think about things from the opposite direction: For what kind of affluent client in your chosen niche would you, with all your personality strengths and flaws, be just the right kind of advisor? The answer should be exactly the same.

Position Yourself as an Expert

In Chapter 5 we'll show you how to effectively grow your assets and attract new affluent clients who fit your ideal client profile. In the meantime, it's worth considering ways of moving your marketing efforts forward once you've chosen your target market niche.

Begin by fully immersing yourself in your niche. Declare yourself as someone who is an expert in the needs of the members of your niche. Your goal is to be first in the minds of members of this community, and that means positioning yourself as the expert who delivers compelling value that niche members won't find anywhere else. There are four steps to such successful positioning:

1. Identify your *compelling value proposition*—the single most important value that you offer to your clients and that sets you apart from your competition.

2. Write your *positioning statement*—a succinct description of your compelling value proposition.

3. Create an *elevator speech*—a brief, persuasive speech that motivates prospective clients to

explore doing business with you.

4. Construct a *call to action*—a specific first step you would like prospective clients to take.

A compelling value proposition goes deeper than your specific skill set. Instead, it is the specific set of financial challenges you are particularly adept at solving. Obviously, it should be in close alignment with the needs of members of your niche. As **Exhibit 3.13** shows, the single most important criterion for the affluent in choosing an advisor is the advisor's overall expertise. Once you determine your real expertise in solving the financial challenges of your clients, you can claim this as the centerpiece of your value proposition and commit to being seen as the expert your clients want.

Next, create a succinct statement of your compelling value proposition. This should be a clear, brief description of the value that you uniquely provide to your select group of clients and prospects and that is designed to meet their precise needs. It's a proclamation that resonates with the members of your niche and acts as a beacon to draw them to you. Two examples are "I help clients in my niche make smart decisions about their money so they can spend more time doing what they love" and "I make work optional for my niche."

Your positioning statement must do each of the following:

1. Provide a strong promise of benefits for your ideal clients
2. Offer to solve a challenge that already exists for these clients

EXHIBIT 3.13	Selection Criteria of Affluent Individuals in Choosing Advisors	
Criterion		**Clients Rating Criterion as Very Important**
Overall expertise of advisor		91.0%
Care advisor takes to identify needs		89.0%
Investment management style		84.1%
Trust in advisor		82.0%
Discretion of advisor		81.1%
Attentiveness of advisor		80.2%
Advisor's desire to establish long-term relationship		74.2%
Reputation of advisor		65.2%
Quality of proposals		55.1%
Quality of presentations		51.9%
Quality of promotional materials		33.9%
Investment performance/track record		26.6%

Source: Russ Alan Prince and David A. Geracioti, *Cultivating the Middle-Class Millionaire*, 2005.
Analysis: CEG Worldwide.

3. Make your offer appear different from and better than your competition's

Above all, your positioning statement must be believable. As a sanity check, make sure your statement reflects what you really do and can do and is something you feel confident and passionate about.

The third step is to craft a compelling "elevator speech"—a statement that effectively communicates your compelling value proposition in the time it takes an elevator to reach its destination, perhaps 15 seconds at most. You can also think of this as the micro-speech you'd give a prospective client at a cocktail party. Make it short, make it passionate, and practice it in front of both other people and a video camera. Once you've said it a hundred times or so it will become second nature and you'll be able to flawlessly deliver it when it counts.

The final step is to construct a call to action. When prospective clients hear your elevator speech and express interest, you must be able to offer them an easy first step toward working with you. In almost every case your call to action will be to have the prospect schedule an initial meeting to explore the possibility of working with you. (We'll say much more about this first meeting in the next chapter.) Here's an example of what you might say:

> "I'd be happy to meet with you for what we call our Discovery Meeting. The purpose of this meeting would be to explore whether we are the right firm to offer you extraordinary value. We work only with a select group of clients for whom we can have a tremendous impact. If we are not the right firm for you, we'd be more than happy to refer you to one that is. Would you like to schedule a Discovery Meeting?"

Pull Clients to You with Credibility Marketing

As you create and refine your positioning statement, elevator speech and call to action, begin to reinforce your status as an expert through a credibility or "pull marketing" program. Ideally, you want to pull clients toward you rather than having to chase after them. In part, this will naturally begin to happen as you build your reputation within your niche and you generate referrals from highly satisfied clients. Simultaneously, however, you want to get your name out there as the financial advisor most qualified to solve the challenges of members of your niche. We recommend these actions:

- **Review your existing marketing materials.** Assess your marketing collateral to see whether it supports your new niche-focused strategy and is in sync with your existing and potential niche clients. Review everything that reflects your brand—logo, letterhead, business cards, brochure, Web site, even the signage on your building—and jettison anything that no longer fits.

- **Write and publish a positioning package.** Create a comprehensive positioning package that describes in detail your firm's mission, history, personnel, fees, strategic alliances, wealth management philosophy and consultative process (described in the next chapter). Your positioning package should be professionally designed and visually appealing and should make clear all the benefits of working with you.

- **Build an effective Web site.** Construct a comprehensive, professional Web site that clearly communicates the special value you offer your niche. Don't skimp here and hire your nephew or simply accept the mass-manufactured Web site that your firm may offer for free. Make sure your site offers an email newsletter, and then send one out to existing and potential clients on a regular basis.

- **Write articles for your niche's trade publications.** Seek out publications that are relevant to your niche, and do your best to get published in them. In addition to asking your niche's COIs what magazines and publications they read, consult titles such as *Writer's Market*, the *Encyclopedia of Associations* and the *Gale Directory of Publications and Broadcast Media*. Your goal should be to publish at least three articles a year of from 750 to 1,500 words. Another possibility is to secure a monthly or bimonthly column in a relevant publication. Have reprints of your published articles or columns readily available for your clients and make them available on your Web site. For pull marketing purposes, trade publications within your niche are far superior to being quoted or published in the local newspaper.

- **Write and publish white papers.** Take what you've learned from your COI interviews and create white papers that address the challenges faced by those in your niche. Ideally, you should combine industry research with your own commentary and recommendations. If you're not a good writer, hire someone to help you. Once finished, distribute your white paper as widely as possible, making it available on your Web site, sending it to publications, and having professional reprints available for clients and potential clients.

■ **Write and publish books.** Having a book or two with your name on it can tremendously increase your credibility, but don't take this on until you have a dozen or so articles or a few white papers under your belt. Writing and having a book published is a major undertaking, one that can all too easily distract you from your core efforts and competencies. Consider working with a professional writer on this.

In addition to these steps, consider researching and contacting media resources to see how feasible it is for you to appear on radio, television or a regular Internet broadcast with an audience relevant to your target market niche. Even if you can't arrange an appearance on a show relevant to your niche, the very fact that you've made appearances on radio, television or broadcast-style Internet will reinforce your position as an expert among both your existing and prospective clients.

In all your marketing efforts, you will need to decide whether to do the work yourself; have an employee or assistant do it; or outsource it to a freelance writer, marketing specialist or advertising agency. Working with outside experts may cost you more, but is also likely to provide the results you want in a timely fashion without distracting you from serving your existing clients and finding new ones who fit squarely into your ideal client profile.

With your understanding in place of which affluent clients to work with and how to attract them to you, it's time to look at how to work with them effectively. We turn to that next.

CHAPTER 4

Strengthen Client Relationships

Strengthen Client Relationships

In Chapter 3 we covered **whom** *you want to attract: affluent clients fitting your ideal client profile. We also discussed the importance of establishing yourself as an expert in order to begin to "pull in" prospective ideal clients.*

Now we will show you *how* to work with these ideal prospects and clients. By using the wealth management consulting process we set out, you'll win new business and "WOW" your clients with an unprecedented level of professional focus and attention.

This chapter will show you how to build such strong client relationships that your clients aren't just satisfied, but are completely loyal to you and absolutely passionate about being your clients. Needless to say, loyal and passionate clients will give you more of their assets to manage, provide referrals for other ideal clients and generally be a pleasure to work with.

We'll begin by explaining why wealth management is far and away the best business model. We'll also briefly consider what to do about your existing clients who don't fit your ideal client profile. We'll then describe the consultative process in detail, including how to create a Total Client Profile by using a tool known as "mind mapping." Finally, we'll cover the mechanics of building a professional network to help deliver the range of advanced planning services that your affluent clients need and expect.

The Wealth Management Business Model

Virtually all financial advisors employ one of two business models:

1. **Investment generalists.** These advisors offer a broad range of investment products and do not specialize in a single type of product. While they conduct brief fact-finding sessions and then offer clients a suite of possible products based on their needs, consulting is not an essential part of their business model. Instead, they are transaction-focused.

2. **Wealth managers.** These advisors take a comprehensive approach to meeting client needs by using a highly consultative approach to construct integrated, personalized solutions.

As you know, many advisors these days *call* themselves "wealth managers." One recent CEG Worldwide study of 2,094 financial advisors showed that 46.3 percent identified themselves as wealth managers, while the remainder (53.7 percent) identified themselves according to their investment orientation, such as financial advisor, investment advisor, investment expert or financial planner. However, the study showed that only 6.6 percent of the advisors actually *are* wealth managers. The remainder, or 93.4 percent, are investment-oriented.

Why do so many advisors want to be *seen* as wealth managers even though they really aren't? Perhaps it's because true wealth managers are, on average, far more successful than investment generalists.

As **Exhibit 4.2** shows, while wealth managers on average have far fewer clients than investment generalists do, their average assets under management or administration are more than twice as great. Even more revealing is the fact that wealth managers, on average, earn more than three times as much as investment generalists ($881,000 vs. $279,000 per year). These, of course, are only averages, and many wealth managers actually do far better than this.

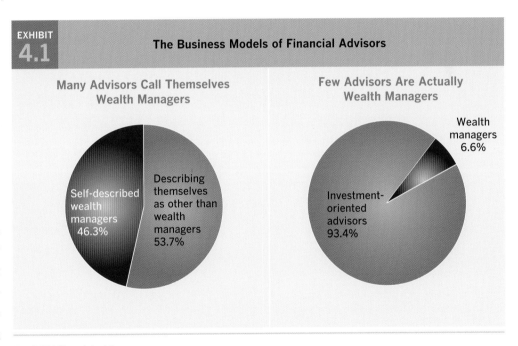

EXHIBIT 4.1 **The Business Models of Financial Advisors**

Many Advisors Call Themselves Wealth Managers

Self-described wealth managers 46.3%

Describing themselves as other than wealth managers 53.7%

Few Advisors Are Actually Wealth Managers

Wealth managers 6.6%

Investment-oriented advisors 93.4%

N = 2,094 financial advisors.
Source: CEG Worldwide, 2007.

A Deeper Look at Wealth Management

In Chapter 3 we discussed the kind of services and the client experience that affluent individuals are looking for. Assuming that the affluent vote with their feet and their pocketbooks, it's clear from **Exhibit 4.2** that wealth management is indeed the business model that affluent clients strongly prefer. Let's take an in-depth look, then, at what wealth management really means.

At its core, wealth management (WM) is comprised of investment consulting (IC) plus advanced planning (AP) plus relationship management (RM). In shorthand:

$$WM = IC + AP + RM$$

As our formula shows, investment consulting is the first element of wealth management. While some advisors turn to other professionals or a TAMP (turnkey asset management provider) to undertake asset allocation and construction of their clients' portfolios, affluent clients expect their primary advisors to be competent at the basics of investment management. Without such basic proficiency, it would be impossible to oversee the activities of other financial professionals and to keep each client's overall financial situation clearly in mind.

The second component is advanced planning, which comprises wealth enhancement (WE), wealth transfer (WT), wealth protection (WP) and charitable planning (CP), as expressed by this formula:

$$AP = WE + WT + WP + CP$$

EXHIBIT 4.2	The Two Business Models Compared	
	Business Model	
	Investment Generalist	**Wealth Manager**
Average assets under administration	$307.8 million	$645.2 million
Average annual net income	$279,000	$881,000
Average number of clients	269.3	101.1

N = 2,094 financial advisors.
Source: CEG Worldwide, 2007.

The intention of advanced planning is to ensure that affluent clients' financial houses are in order so that they can achieve their dreams. As with investment consulting, its significance directly flows from what's important to affluent clients.

Thus, the various components of advanced planning speak to key concerns, including (1) income taxes (wealth enhancement aims to produce the best possible investment returns consistent with the client's risk tolerance while minimizing tax impacts), (2) the desire to efficiently transfer wealth to successive generations, and (3) risk mitigation through wealth protection (either eliminating risk entirely or transferring it to insurance companies or other parties). Additionally, as we noted in Chapter 3, more than 25 percent of affluent clients are concerned with charitable planning. By combining these four advanced planning areas with investment consulting, advisors address the spectrum of major financial concerns of their affluent clients.

Most advisors who claim to be wealth managers often provide only investment consulting. They provide any additional services on a reactive basis. Offering advanced planning services therefore represents a major opportunity to differentiate yourself. But don't overpromise. For example, you must already have an extended expert network (as we describe later in this chapter) in place or well under way before you can effectively provide the range of advanced planning services.

The final component that ties wealth management together is relationship management (RM). This, in turn, consists of CRM (client relationship management) and ENRM (expert network relationship management). This is our shorthand:

$$RM = CRM + ENRM$$

Client relationship management in the wealth management model means forging in-depth, collaborative and consultative client relationships. But since affluent clients these days recognize that no one can be an expert in everything, they want their primary advisors to work closely with the experts that they already have on board (such as their accountants and lawyers) as well as additional experts that their advisors will bring to the party from their own networks.

Relationship management involves three key tasks:

1. Building deep client relationships that will allow you to fully understand your clients' most important financial challenges and dreams. This, in turn, will enable you to effectively meet all their needs. The best means for building these types of relationships is the consultative process.

2. Assembling and managing a network of your own experts (including lawyers, insurance experts and so on) so that you can bring to bear the exact expertise that your clients need.

3. Working with the professional advisors your affluent clients already have, such as attorneys and accountants, as well as other financial advisors managing other parts of their finances.

As a wealth manager, you'll become what your affluent clients really want you to be: their personal chief financial officer, someone who helps them think through their challenges while working with them collaboratively to determine and implement optimal solutions. We turn next to using the consultative process to build exactly this type of relationship.

Releasing Inappropriate Clients

To succeed as a wealth manager, you need to work with fewer but wealthier clients. This means that you'll have to let go of those clients who are not part of your target market niche or who otherwise do not fit your ideal client profile.

Once you have determined whom you should let go, you may still find yourself reluctant to actually release certain clients, especially if they've been with you for a long time. But the truth is, if they aren't the right clients for you, then you're almost certainly not the right advisor for them, and keeping them on as clients is actually doing them a disservice. These clients will receive more value by working with someone else, perhaps someone who is newer in the business or who specializes in clients just like them. When such clients are turned over to a more appropriate advisor, the typical response is "Thank you for referring me elsewhere." They are quite happy to get the services and value they need from the right advisor.

What's the best way to release clients? As **Exhibit 4.3** shows, you have five choices. The most common method—"quiet filing" clients—is the worst possible choice because it rarely works and ultimately amounts to just ignoring the problem. The best possible method is to "bundle" the clients you wish to let go of and sell them to another advisor.

Such sales are increasingly common, and a number of consulting firms specialize in facilitating these kinds of transactions. An earn-out will often be part of the deal. You might receive a certain percentage of the previous year's revenue associated with the sold clients, plus an amount equal to that over the next one to two years. The downside here is that it takes time and energy to value your clients and then find an outside advisor whom you feel good about and who is willing to pay a fair price. The upside is that this method truly takes inappropriate clients off your plate and can put them in the hands of an advisor better able to service them.

Continued on following page

EXHIBIT 4.3	**Five Methods for Releasing Clients**		
Method	**Pros**	**Cons**	**The Upshot**
"Quiet file" the clients	Quick, easy, immediate and inexpensive; needs no client buy-in	Problem clients rarely "fade away"; long-term compliance and legal risks; inconsistent with positioning yourself as an expert	Most advisors default to this, but this is *not* the recommended course of action
Hire a junior advisor within your office to service the clients	Relatively easy to get client buy-in; advisor retains revenue stream and ultimate relationship	Must train, supervise and pay salary of new advisor; does not fundamentally address inappropriate nature of clients	Not a silver bullet, since doesn't address clients' fundamental inappropriateness
Transfer the clients to an advisor in your office	Favored by branch managers; advisor may retain a portion of ongoing revenue stream	Again, does not address clients' inappropriate nature; clients may demand original advisor's attention	Branch managers often eager to help facilitate this
Sell "bundled" clients to advisor in another office	Truly addresses inappropriate clients; advisor receives immediate and perhaps earn-out revenue	Takes time and focus to value clients, negotiate a deal and assist in transfer process	Best possible option; consulting firms available to facilitate
Directly, formally and carefully fire clients	Avoids potential compliance and legal issues; gets rid of problem clients	Requires thoughtful and delicate handling; legal and compliance issues must be thoroughly addressed	A last resort for problem clients who refuse to be transferred or sold

By releasing less-than-ideal and otherwise inappropriate clients, you'll free up a tremendous amount of productive time to focus on attracting new clients and servicing existing clients, and you'll also dramatically improve your self-image. It's critical, however, that you release these clients in a careful, respectful way. Put yourself in the shoes of those whom you'll be releasing. Ask yourself what kind of treatment you would want in this situation, from timely notice to a sensible explanation of why it is better for everyone involved to a handwritten thank-you note for the business that you provided over the years.

Real-World Success Story: Releasing Inappropriate Clients While Setting Higher Fees

For many advisors, the coaching program isn't about staging a turnaround—it's about taking their already established businesses to a higher level of success. Take Ron Wyatt. A senior vice president with Wachovia Securities in Pittsburgh, Wyatt has introduced a minimum account size ($1 million) and minimum fee ($9,000) and now brings in roughly $45,000 in fee-only business per month on average, up from approximately $33,000 before the program (he also generates roughly $50,000 annually from mutual fund and variable annuity trails).

Meanwhile, he's adopted a key coaching program strategy of working with only larger accounts that he can serve profitably, while transferring smaller clients to other advisors. Guided by CEG Worldwide's advice, Wyatt transferred 56 of his roughly 140 clients to another Wachovia advisor but will keep nearly all the revenue those clients generate during the next two years. "That gives me a two-year window to implement the coaching program's strategies, without having my fees suffer in the process," he says.

What's more, existing clients' reaction to Wyatt's fee increase has been overwhelmingly positive. Wyatt credits that success in part to CEG Worldwide's Consultative Client Management Process designed to determine clients' most important financial needs and attitudes and work in close consultation with them to achieve their goals. "My clients recognize that I'm now going to serve them on a deeper level that brings more value to their lives," he says. "Nearly everyone I've approached about the new fee structure has accepted it."

The Wealth Management Consulting Process

The wealth management consulting process is a potent, field-tested way to strengthen client relationships and ensure that your affluent clients' needs are fully met. As a wealth manager, you'll leverage two primary tools:

1. The Consultative Client Management (CCM) Process, consisting of a series of five different client meetings. Each is designed to foster trust, grow your relationships, and delight your prospective and existing clients. At the same time, they will provide you with numerous opportunities to gain additional assets, provide additional services and receive referrals for more clients who fit your ideal client profile. The meetings of the CCM Process are shown on the left side of **Exhibit 4.4.** As part of the CCM Process, you will use mind mapping to create a Total Client Profile, a comprehensive description of seven key areas of your client's life. Using the Total Client Profile, you will create an investment plan, and later on you will create a broader wealth management plan.

2. The expert network that will provide you with the top-end expertise that your clients need. The network and its activities are shown at the right side of **Exhibit 4.4**.

We will look at the CCM Process first. Every step of this process is replicable, enabling you to consistently provide every prospective and existing client with the same high-quality experience. Knowing that they are part of a refined and well-thought-out process will bolster their confidence in you, making it more likely that they'll refer their qualified friends (who they know will also receive a top-notch experience) as well as give you additional business and remain loyal over time.

We will now take you through that client experience, beginning with your first contact with the prospect, the Discovery Meeting.

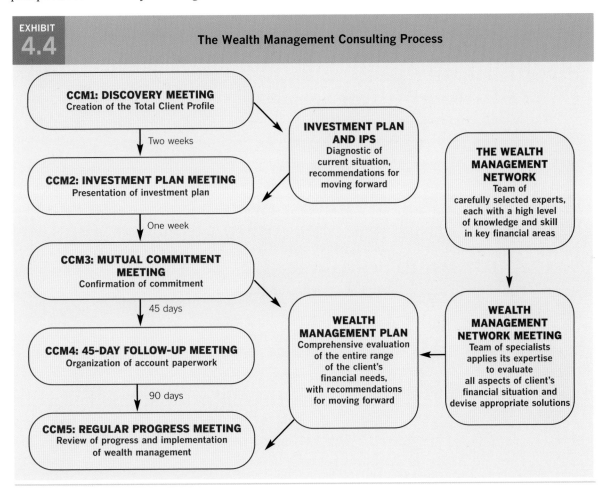

EXHIBIT 4.4

The Wealth Management Consulting Process

CCM1: DISCOVERY MEETING
Creation of the Total Client Profile

Two weeks

CCM2: INVESTMENT PLAN MEETING
Presentation of investment plan

One week

CCM3: MUTUAL COMMITMENT MEETING
Confirmation of commitment

45 days

CCM4: 45-DAY FOLLOW-UP MEETING
Organization of account paperwork

90 days

CCM5: REGULAR PROGRESS MEETING
Review of progress and implementation of wealth management

INVESTMENT PLAN AND IPS
Diagnostic of current situation, recommendations for moving forward

THE WEALTH MANAGEMENT NETWORK
Team of carefully selected experts, each with a high level of knowledge and skill in key financial areas

WEALTH MANAGEMENT PLAN
Comprehensive evaluation of the entire range of the client's financial needs, with recommendations for moving forward

WEALTH MANAGEMENT NETWORK MEETING
Team of specialists applies its expertise to evaluate all aspects of client's financial situation and devise appropriate solutions

Source: CEG Worldwide.

CCM1: Discovery Meeting

As its name suggests, this is your opportunity to discover everything that is financially important to your client. These are your objectives for the Discovery Meeting:

- To immediately establish trust by positioning yourself as an expert
- To differentiate yourself from your competition through your in-depth, holistic process
- To uncover the prospect's most important financial issues and to determine his or her high-net-worth personality
- To collect all information necessary to assess client suitability
- If appropriate, to create a Total Client Profile, which you will use to craft an investment plan and a wealth management plan
- To begin to position yourself as the client's personal chief financial officer

To ensure that the Discovery Meeting is as productive as possible, send a letter ahead of time confirming the date and time of the meeting and listing the information you'd like the prospect to bring to the meeting, such as account statements and recent income tax returns. In addition, you should also prepare an agenda for the meeting.

The experience starts the moment the prospect walks into your office. Remember, everything the prospect sees, hears or otherwise notices reflects directly on you. To begin, your receptionist or assistant should greet the prospect formally, by name, and offer a beverage. This shows respect and signals that you are well-prepared.

If you have a waiting room, make sure it is *not* filled with the standard variety of financial magazines. We refer to these as "financial pornography" because they only excite and confuse clients and don't support what you are trying to accomplish as a wealth manager. Instead, since one of your primary goals is to help affluent clients achieve their dreams, make available a variety of

Overview of Discovery Meeting Steps

1. Every employee greets the prospect by name, using a formal greeting.
2. Acknowledge the prospect's desire to explore working together.
3. Explain how you will conduct the meeting.
4. Conduct the Total Client Profile interview, creating a mind map as you conduct the interview.
5. Assess whether you can add substantial value to the prospect's situation.
6. Gain a precommitment from the prospect to move forward.
7. Describe the next steps in the process.
8. Schedule the next meeting.
9. Send confirmation of the next meeting.

lifestyle magazines focused on subjects that are of interest to your niche such as wine, golf, travel or real estate. If you have a television monitor in the waiting room, don't tune it to a financial news channel, since you don't want to waste the first part of your meeting calming your prospect's fears or explaining why the latest investment fad is irrelevant. Instead, show a travel channel or play lifestyle-oriented DVDs to set the right frame of mind.

When you greet the prospect (or existing client), remember that you are not trying to sell anything but, rather, that you are *qualifying* the individual as a potential client. Speaking in a respectful but not obsequious manner, say something like this:

> "I'm excited that you're here today to explore whether we are the right firm for you. We work with a limited number of successful families—those for whom we can have a substantial positive impact. I would like to ask you a series of questions, and, based on your answers, if it appears unlikely that we can make a strong positive impact for you, I'll be more than happy to refer you to another firm that might better fit your needs."

> ## Critical Success Factors for the Discovery Meeting
>
> - **Be confident.** Approach the Discovery Meeting from the perspective of whether this prospect is really appropriate for your firm, in terms of both overall match to your ideal client profile and profitability potential.
> - **Be focused.** The meeting should be extremely tight and focused and not run more than 1.5 hours. Don't make it an endurance test.
> - **Be efficient.** Recognize that the affluent already have more than enough friends. What they often really have is a shortage of time. They want professionals who are extremely efficient and effective.
> - **Be well-practiced.** Creating a Total Client Profile using a mind map takes a bit of practice. Ask your co-workers, family members and friends if you can practice on them first.

Then explain how you will conduct the meeting and briefly review the agenda. By the end of the meeting you should be able to assess whether you can add substantial value to the prospect's situation. If you feel that you can, describe the next steps and ask for a commitment from the prospect to move forward. If you get this commitment, schedule the meeting then and there and shortly thereafter send a written confirmation of the date and time.

Creating the Total Client Profile

At the heart of the Discovery Meeting is the creation of the Total Client Profile. (See **Exhibit 4.5** for an overview of this process.) Your goal is to discover everything you possibly can about your prospective client in seven key areas:

1. **Values.** What's truly important to your prospect about money and finances? Here, and throughout the process, have questions prepared that enable you to quickly go deeper to find out how the prospect truly feels. For example, a typical answer to "What's most important to you about your finances?" is "Financial security." Because this doesn't actually reveal very much, you can then follow up with a "second-order" question such as "What specifically about financial security is of most concern to you?" The prospect might respond, "Taking care of my family's health and well-being" or "Maintaining my lifestyle through retirement." These specific responses will enable you to do a better job for your prospective client.

2. **Goals.** What does the prospect want to achieve over the long run? When does he or she want to retire? How about college for any children? What about travel or a second career? What other dreams does the prospect have?

3. **Relationships.** Who really counts for your prospect? Whom does the prospect love? Who is important to your prospect, including non-family members and even pets?

4. **Assets.** In order to address the prospect's entire financial picture, you must find out what the prospect's assets are, and where and how they are held. This includes real estate, home businesses, brokerage accounts, retirement plans and so on. (Ask the prospect in advance of the meeting to bring tax returns and account records and have an assistant photocopy the records during your meeting.) Note that you ask about assets fourth, not first. This reflects your understanding that there are things more important to the prospect than money.

5. **Advisors.** Whom does the prospect rely on for advice, from CPAs and attorneys to insurance agents and other financial advisors? Find out what has worked—and what has not—in your prospect's relationships with these other advisors.

6. **Process.** How does the prospect prefer to work with his or her advisors? Once the prospect has expressed a preference, be prepared to honor that choice for the rest of your relationship. If the prospect only wants to be contacted by email and never by phone, then that's what you must do.

7. **Interests.** What are the prospect's hobbies, sports and leisure activities, charitable and philanthropic involvements, religious and spiritual proclivities, and children's schools and activities? If you share an interest with your prospective client, over time you can leverage this interest to build further intimacy.

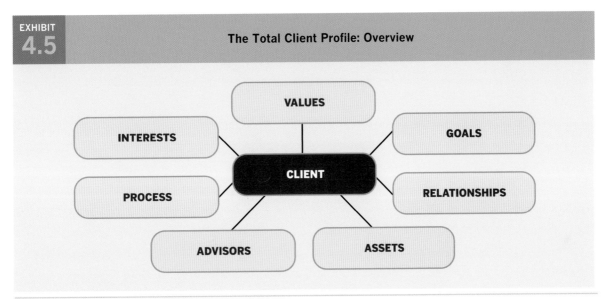

EXHIBIT 4.5 — The Total Client Profile: Overview

Source: CEG Worldwide.

As you can see, your inquiry into who the prospect really is goes much further than the fact-finding process used by most advisors, which is typically limited to assets, net worth, time horizon, investment goals and risk tolerance. While these subjects are clearly important and need to be covered, they do little to reveal what really matters most to the individual (or couple) in front of you.

We recommend that you use an interview guide to ensure that you thoroughly cover all seven areas. You can construct such a guide yourself, or alternatively, CEG Worldwide has put together an in-depth interview guide and scripts that we make available to advisors in our coaching programs.

We also recommend that you record your interview with a digital voice recorder. Let the prospect know that you will be recording the session so that you can stay fully engaged without worrying about missing some vital piece of information. (You can also assure the prospect that whether or not he or she becomes your client, any recorded information will remain absolutely confidential.)

As you ask questions in each area, you'll do two things. First, you'll listen—really deeply listen—to the prospect's responses, both so that he or she *feels heard* and so that you actually *have heard* what was said. In our hyper-sales-focused industry, far too many advisors are better at talking than at listening, but it's in the listening—the open and unhurried receiving of information—that real relationship develops.

Second, you'll create a mind map on an unlined piece of paper or flip chart. Begin by putting in the prospect's name (or both names for a couple) in the center, and then draw connecting lines and text bubbles for each of the seven main areas of inquiry. As you move through your questions, capture the prospect's responses in the appropriate places, using any kind of graphic elements you like, not just words. Connect responses with lines when they relate to one another to illustrate the interconnectedness of the various parts of the prospect's life. Done well, a mind map will stimulate thorough responses, trigger new and deeper questions, and capture relevant information that randomly arises. Exhibit 4.6 provides an example of a completed Total Client Profile.

There are many advantages to using mind mapping over traditional note taking:

- It helps you to drill down to the prospect's key issues faster and more accurately.
- It captures information quickly, yet in a highly organized format.
- It makes it easy to link and cross-reference very different, yet connected, pieces of the prospect's financial picture.
- It involves prospects more deeply in the discovery process, motivating them to provide you with all the information you need to complete their profiles.
- It provides a basis for moving forward with clear goals and next steps.
- It provides you with a document that is fast and easy to review.

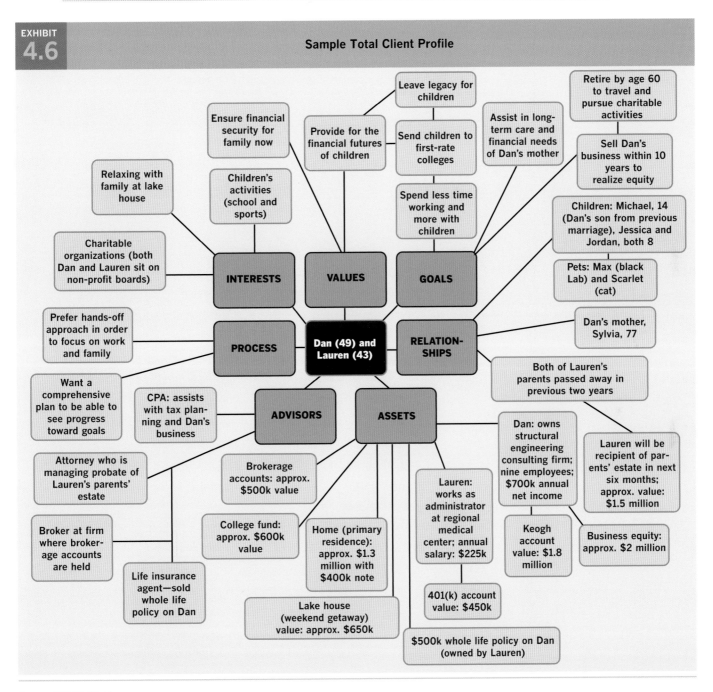

EXHIBIT 4.6

Sample Total Client Profile

Dan (49) and Lauren (43)

INTERESTS
- Relaxing with family at lake house
- Charitable organizations (both Dan and Lauren sit on non-profit boards)
- Children's activities (school and sports)

VALUES
- Ensure financial security for family now
- Leave legacy for children
- Provide for the financial futures of children
- Send children to first-rate colleges
- Spend less time working and more with children

GOALS
- Assist in long-term care and financial needs of Dan's mother
- Retire by age 60 to travel and pursue charitable activities
- Sell Dan's business within 10 years to realize equity

RELATIONSHIPS
- Children: Michael, 14 (Dan's son from previous marriage), Jessica and Jordan, both 8
- Pets: Max (black Lab) and Scarlet (cat)
- Dan's mother, Sylvia, 77
- Both of Lauren's parents passed away in previous two years
- Lauren will be recipient of parents' estate in next six months; approx. value: $1.5 million

PROCESS
- Prefer hands-off approach in order to focus on work and family
- Want a comprehensive plan to be able to see progress toward goals

ADVISORS
- CPA: assists with tax planning and Dan's business
- Attorney who is managing probate of Lauren's parents' estate
- Broker at firm where brokerage accounts are held
- Life insurance agent—sold whole life policy on Dan

ASSETS
- Brokerage accounts: approx. $500k value
- College fund: approx. $600k value
- Home (primary residence): approx. $1.3 million with $400k note
- Lake house (weekend getaway) value: approx. $650k
- Lauren: works as administrator at regional medical center; annual salary: $225k
- 401(k) account value: $450k
- $500k whole life policy on Dan (owned by Lauren)
- Dan: owns structural engineering consulting firm; nine employees; $700k annual net income
- Keogh account value: $1.8 million
- Business equity: approx. $2 million

Real-World Success Story: Conducting Effective Discovery Interviews

Advisor Chris Gardner, president of Syracuse, New York-based FMF&E Wealth Management, saw his assets under management grow from $50 million to $65 million—a 30 percent increase—in just the first eight months of his participation in the coaching program.

Fueling that impressive growth was a change in focus, what Gardner calls a seismic shift in how he communicates with prospective clients. Rather than spend introductory meetings talking about investments ad nauseam as he's done in the past, Gardner now focuses entirely on asking targeted questions expertly designed to uncover the prospect's financial attitudes, issues and goals. "I now spend most of my meetings listening to the person in front of me instead of talking at them," he says. "As a result I've become a true expert in understanding what my clients really want and tailoring solutions for them."

- It is an excellent starting point for brainstorming solutions with members of your network of professional advisors.

The information you gather during the mind-mapping process will tell you whether the prospect fits your ideal client profile. If you discover that there is not a good match, then inform the prospect and move on. If it is a good match, then you'll have all the information needed to move to the next step: creating an investment plan and a wealth management plan.

CCM2: Investment Plan Meeting

The Investment Plan Meeting should take place about two weeks after the Discovery Meeting. Here, you'll present a detailed, actionable investment plan (along with an investment policy statement, or IPS) that will serve as a road map that maximizes the probability of achieving everything that's financially important to the prospect. It will also further establish you as an expert in the eyes of the prospect. During this meeting, you'll also continue to build your personal relationship with the prospect.

Your primary task in advance of the Investment Plan Meeting is to create the prospect's investment plan. A well-designed investment plan serves the following important purposes:

- **It provides you with an opportunity to clarify and solidify the prospect's goals.** Drawn from the information gathered during the Discovery Meeting, the investment plan documents all seven areas from the prospect's Total Client Profile. Often the most critical area for investment decisions concerns the prospect's financial goals. By putting these goals in writing, the investment plan ensures that both you and the prospect are completely clear about this vital area.

- **It provides long-term discipline for the prospect's investment decision making.** A well-drafted plan helps ensure that rational analysis is the basis for the prospect's investment decisions, making the prospect less likely to act on emotional responses to short-term or one-time events.

■ **It promotes clear communication.** Because it clarifies the issues that are most important to the prospect and the approaches that you will use, the investment plan can prevent misunderstandings that might otherwise arise.

■ **It provides you with an opportunity to "WOW" the prospect.** The investment plan demonstrates that you are extremely thoughtful in your approach to solving the prospect's financial challenges. The document reflects your thorough preparation, systematic strategy and close attention to detail.

Note that you are creating an *investment* plan here, not a *financial* plan. It's true that astute financial planning can play a crucial role in the overall wealth management process, which is why you will use your team of experts to create a wealth management plan later on in the consultative process. But most advisors, especially at this early stage, find it extremely difficult to execute a financial plan either well or profitably. By positioning yourself as a financial planner, you are effectively communicating to prospects that you are an expert in all aspects of financial services, and this is simply impossible.

In contrast, an actionable, comprehensive investment plan communicates a very different message: that you are primarily focused on the one aspect of their finances that many affluent prospects are most concerned about—preserving their wealth. Only after the investment plan is in place will you turn your attention to other aspects of the prospect's financial situation, and you will do this in concert with experts in those other areas.

The investment plan itself should be divided into two parts:

1. **An executive summary of your investment consulting work and recommendations for the prospect.** This will provide an overview of the prospect's Total Client Profile, your consulting process and your investment recommendations. It should also include brief descriptions of your fees, as well as your firm's background and investment philosophy.

2. **An investment policy statement.** The IPS should delve into substantial detail as to your investing approach and strategic portfolio management process, thereby demonstrating to the

Overview of Investment Plan Meeting Steps

1. Greet the prospect by name. Reinforce some aspect of his or her high-net-worth personality.
2. Set the stage for the meeting.
3. Outline the agenda and describe the remaining steps of the Consultative Client Management Process.
4. Walk the prospect through the investment plan.
5. Ask for a commitment for moving forward.
6. Solicit and address concerns about the plan.
7. Set the stage for the wealth management plan.
8. Close the meeting.
9. Send confirmation of the next meeting.

prospective client the thoughtfulness of your firm's overall investment process. It should also provide summaries of the returns of key indexes and of a range of hypothetical portfolios that your firm recommends (rather than addressing the prospective client's individual situation).

There's no need to walk the prospect through the IPS in detail. Most high-net-worth personality types—with the exception of the Accumulator, the Gambler and the Innovator (who make the worst clients for wealth managers—see Chapter 3)—won't be interested in the details of your IPS. But all your clients will be glad that you do in fact have an IPS. (You should review your IPS on an annual basis to make any necessary changes and make sure that it addresses all regulatory requirements.)

As shown below, the mechanics of the Investment Plan Meeting are similar to those of the Discovery Meeting, from how you greet the prospect and cover the agenda to how you wrap up the meeting. The core of the meeting, of course, is presenting the investment plan. Go through it in detail and respond to any questions or concerns.

After you discuss the investment plan, ask the prospect for a commitment to move forward. You are not, at this point, looking to have the client actually invest—to actually write a check. Remember, you are using a consultative approach. It is not your job to persuade the prospect to do something, but to help the prospect understand what the right thing to do is. Then, as the prospect-turned-client's personal chief financial officer, your job is to execute the plan. So you want the prospect to take the time to really think things through. Many prospects are ready to invest at this second meeting, but you should insist that they take the materials back home and then return for a Mutual Commitment Meeting. At that point, if they are committed to achieving their goals vis-à-vis the investment plan, you will commit to their success where both parties can make the necessary commitment and execute the required paperwork.

After you've received the commitment, set the stage for the wealth management plan. Explain that investments are only the foundation of the entire financial picture and that once the prospect becomes a client you will work with your network of expert specialists to identify those areas beyond investments where additional work may be needed.

CCM3: Mutual Commitment Meeting

Schedule the Mutual Commitment Meeting about one week after the Investment Plan Meeting. At this meeting the prospect will become a client.

This meeting has two objectives. The first is to make the mutual commitment to work together to achieve the client's goals and values. In addition to verbally ascertaining this, you will assist the client in executing the documents necessary to implement the investment plan. The second objective is to seek qualified referrals from your new or existing client.

To get ready for the Mutual Commitment Meeting, prepare the paperwork necessary to execute the investment plan's recommendations. Review the investment plan and have a copy available for the meeting. Also review the client's entire file, including the Total Client Profile and your notes of any questions or concerns raised during the Investment Plan Meeting. Ensure that you're completely up to speed on the prospect's situation and investment plan so you can confidently and competently answer any further questions. And, of course, as with all meetings, prepare an agenda.

After greeting the prospect, collect and address any questions. After this, let the prospect know that you're excited about the progress you're making together and ask whether he or she is ready to move forward, become your client and set the investment plan in motion. To expedite the process, have all the paperwork prepared with "sign here" stickers attached in appropriate places. Take the time needed to explain all paperwork. This is also when you will collect any checks, as appropriate.

Once all the documents have been executed, pause for a moment to congratulate the client. Say something like this:

> "You should be commended for moving forward. Congratulations on taking an extremely important step toward securing your financial future and achieving all the things that are important to you."

Explain to your client that some "buyer's remorse" is not uncommon at this point, especially if he or she is used to relying on the financial media for investment information and perspectives. Encourage your new client to ignore the financial media, if possible, or to view it merely as entertainment. Instead, the client should focus on making wise financial decisions—such as working with you—and sticking with a long-term plan for achieving all that is important in his or her financial life.

You may also want to talk to your new client a bit about the concentrated nature of investment gains. Explain that it will be easier to stay the course over the long run if he or she understands that the uneven nature of investment gains is an unavoidable part of attaining investment goals. Missing even short periods can result in dramatically lower returns over time than staying consistently invested all the time. Let the client know to expect down periods as well as up periods and that worrying about every little rise and dip will only lead to making the kind of mistakes that it's your job to help avoid.

Now that your prospect is a client, you should also begin to leverage the relationship by implementing the referral process. Since your new client trusts you with his or her financial future, the client is usually quite willing to help you out by providing the names of qualified prospects in your target market. You simply have to ask. State the kind of individual you are looking for, and ask your new client whether he or she knows anyone who fits the bill. If so, ask for help in contacting this individual.

As you close the meeting, explain that the 45-Day Follow-up Meeting is next. Schedule it about six weeks out. One of the main objectives of that meeting will be to help the new client get organized, so ask the client to save all paperwork and bring it to the meeting. Reassure the client that even if some of the paperwork seems confusing or overwhelming, you and your staff will certainly help with all of it. Then close the meeting by acknowledging that you're glad that you can play an important role in helping your client achieve all that is important to him or her.

Overview of Mutual Commitment Meeting Steps

1. Greet the prospect by name. Reinforce some aspect of his or her high-net-worth personality.
2. Collect all questions and then address them.
3. Execute the documents.
4. Congratulate the client.
5. Caution the client about "buyer's remorse."
6. Explain the concentrated nature of investment gains.
7. Implement the referral process.
8. Close the meeting.
9. Send confirmation of the next meeting.

CCM4: 45-Day Follow-up Meeting

So much paperwork is generated when money is transferred, especially when multiple accounts are involved, that it's quite easy for your client to become inundated in the weeks following the investment plan's implementation. The 45-Day Follow-up Meeting allows you to help the client understand and organize all this financial paperwork. At the same time, it provides you with an opportunity to impress your new client with the quality of your service and gives you a second opportunity to obtain qualified referrals.

To prepare for the meeting, create a tabbed notebook with sections for the investment plan overview, the investment policy statement, the wealth management plan, brokerage statements, your regular progress reports, your newsletter (if you produce one) and miscellaneous communications. Emphasize the long-term nature of your relationship by designing the notebook to accommodate a minimum of five years' worth of paperwork.

After you greet the client and settle down, begin by gathering and responding to any questions. You may want to say, "What has happened since we last met?" After answering or otherwise addressing any questions, dive into the paperwork. Briefly explain what each tabbed section in the notebook is for, and place all the documents in the appropriate sections. As you do so, show the client how to read and understand each document.

Many portfolio management software programs annualize returns even for short periods, and your client will no doubt notice these returns as you're helping to organize the paperwork. If the market did well during the 45 days since the client began working with you, the annualization of the returns will make you look like a genius. On the other hand, if the market is down, the negative returns will make the client wonder why he or she is paying you.

> **Overview of 45-Day Follow-up Meeting Steps**
>
> 1. Greet the client by name. Reinforce some aspect of his or her high-net-worth personality.
> 2. Gather and respond to questions.
> 3. Organize the notebook.
> 4. Place short-term progress into a long-term perspective.
> 5. Ask for referrals.
> 6. Set up the next meeting.
> 7. Send confirmation of the next meeting.

We recommend that you turn this into a learning opportunity, using it as a real-world illustration of the irrelevancy of short-term returns. Explain it like this:

> "What's really important is not investment performance over any isolated period, but achieving your goals over your lifetime. What has happened in the last 45 days has little to do with achieving your goals, because in the long run, the only way to achieve your goals is to make smart decisions about your money. In the short term, no one can know with any accuracy how the market will move. But in the long term, by making prudent decisions, we can maximize the probability of your success."

Before closing the meeting, ask the client for referrals of qualified prospects, as you did in the Mutual Commitment Meeting. Again, simply describe the type of person who would most benefit from your services and ask whether he or she knows anyone who fits this profile. Then schedule the first Regular Progress Meeting. We recommend that these meetings take place on a systematic basis based on the preference the client indicated during your discussion of process during the Discovery Meeting. Confirm the client's preference, and schedule appropriately.

CCM5: Regular Progress Meetings

Regular Progress Meetings give you an opportunity to do three things. First, they let you review your client's progress toward meeting his or her goals. You can answer any questions your client has and help put his or her mind at ease, especially during difficult market climates.

Second, these meetings allow you to continue to build and deepen the client-advisor relationship. You can stay on top of what's happening in your client's life, and you can also continue to gather qualified referrals and additional assets. Ultimately, you want to build such a close relationship and do such a good job for all your clients that they become your marketing apostles.

Third, these meetings give you the opportunity to present and then execute a comprehensive wealth management plan. The plan will contain a range of recommendations designed to meet specific financial challenges, each prioritized according to the impact it can have on the client's life.

In the first Regular Progress Meeting you'll present your client with the third part of the wealth management plan, the advanced planning plan. In most cases you'll rely on your professional network of advisors, described later in this chapter, to analyze your client's situation and make the appropriate recommendations. Every advanced planning plan should deal with four key areas of the client's financial life beyond his or her investments:

1. **Wealth enhancement** aims to produce the best possible investment returns consistent with the client's level of risk tolerance while minimizing the tax impact on those returns.

2. **Wealth transfer** intends to facilitate the most tax-efficient way to pass assets to succeeding generations, and to do so in a way that meets the client's wishes.

3. **Wealth protection** is aimed at protecting the client's wealth against potential creditors, litigants, children's spouses and potential ex-spouses, as well as protecting the client against catastrophic loss.

4. **Charitable gifting** helps fulfill the client's charitable goals and can often support efforts in each of the other three areas.

None of these areas stands in isolation from the rest. Wealth protection, for example, is often intertwined with wealth transfer needs. The major advantage of the wealth management plan is that it enables you to deal with each area systematically while maintaining an integrated approach to the client's overall financial picture.

The mechanics of the Regular Progress Meetings are straightforward. Walk through your agenda and then ask the client whether he or she has any items or questions to add to it. Since your progress report will probably answer most of your client's questions, refrain from immediately answering any questions or concerns at this time.

Next, inquire about any major changes in the client's personal or financial life. You might say, "What have you been doing since we last got together?" If you need to drill deeper, ask, "Has anything happened in your life since our last meeting that affects your finances and that I should know about?" Look for things like job or career changes, births of children or grandchildren, divorces or deaths in the family, and anything else that might require modifying the investment plan or wealth management plan.

Overview of the First Regular Progress Meeting

1. Greet the prospect by name. Reinforce some aspect of his or her high-net-worth personality.
2. Walk through the agenda.
3. Ask about major changes in the client's personal or financial life.
4. Present the third part of the wealth management plan, the advanced planning plan.
5. Discuss and prioritize action items in the wealth management plan.
6. Answer any additional questions.
7. Ask for additional assets and referrals.
8. Schedule the next Regular Progress Meeting.
9. Send out confirmation of the next meeting.

You'll then present the advanced planning plan. Go through each of the four sections at a high level and point out the highest priority items. Discuss in general terms the particular financial items your client faces and how your recommended solutions would address these. When you've moved through the whole plan, discuss each recommended action, providing as much detail as the client needs to make a decision about moving forward on that item. Your job here is to help coach the client to make one of three choices with respect to each recommendation: drop it, defer it or do it.

Take complete notes of the client's response to each recommendation. As you wrap up this part of the Regular Progress Meeting, summarize the next steps for each recommendation.

Next ask your client whether there are any further questions about the wealth management plan. After answering these questions, ask for referrals of qualified prospects and also inquire as to whether he or she has any additional assets for you to manage. Before ending the meeting, schedule the next Regular Progress Meeting.

Subsequent Regular Progress Meetings will follow the same agenda, with several differences. Instead of presenting the advanced planning plan for the first time, you'll review the client's progress relative to both it and the investment plan. You'll also educate the client on particularly relevant aspects of the advanced planning plan and investment plan, making sure that high-priority items remain prominent in your client's mind. If a complex wealth management solution—such as a family limited partnership—is on the table, it can be very helpful to bring in the appropriate expert from your professional network to discuss the issue directly with the client.

Building Your Professional Network

By combining the Consultative Client Management Process with your investment management skills, you'll be fully positioned to meet the investment needs of your affluent clients. But to be a successful wealth manager, you need to address the totality of your clients' financial challenges with the best possible strategies, services and products. This is something that you can't do alone, because no one person can be an expert in the entire range of advanced planning needs and solutions. Instead, you'll build a network of specialists, experts who have deep knowledge in the four advanced planning specialties.

Fortunately—unlike in the old days—to offer complete wealth management services you won't need to actually hire an entire team of specialists and provide them office space, equipment, support services and regular paychecks. Instead, you can put together a virtual team of free-agent experts who are unrestricted by geography and available to work on a strictly as-needed basis. Wealth managers today are able to offer first-rate expertise to their clients by drawing from a nationwide pool of experts, which offers tremendous advantages. And because these experts are free agents (independent contractors), you won't need to pay for their overhead but instead will pay for their expertise only when you use it.

Exhibit 4.8 shows a sample professional network. The network that you create will in part depend on your target affluent niche, since different types of affluent clients have different needs. At a minimum, though, your network should include a private client lawyer and a high-end insurance specialist.

Critical Success Factors for Regular Progress Meetings

- **Be prepared.** You need to know exactly what's going on with the investment account as well as with any current activity related to implementing recommendations from the wealth management plan. If there have been any major changes since your last meeting, notify the client in advance so that there are no surprises.
- **Have timely information.** Always use the most up-to-date information possible, e.g., the previous quarter's closing statements.
- **Reinforce the long-term perspective.** Remind the client of the importance of maintaining a long-term perspective to stay on track and achieve important goals, even when short-term investment performance is down.
- **Keep your edge.** It's easy to fall into the trap of routine when conducting Regular Progress Meetings. You owe it to your client and yourself to deliver a world-class experience every time.

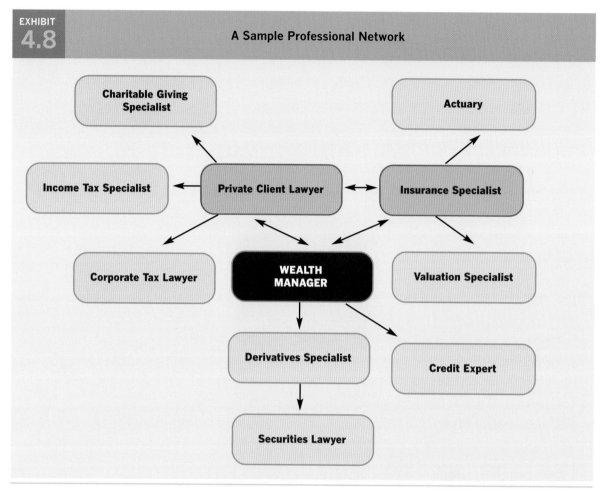

EXHIBIT 4.8

A Sample Professional Network

Source: CEG Worldwide.

The private client lawyer is probably the single most important member of your network, as he or she will address tax, estate planning and legal needs—all critical areas for solving the challenges of wealthy clients. Note that private client lawyers are *not* the trust and estate lawyers employed by private banks or life insurance companies. Instead, they are typically partners at high-end boutique firms. Your insurance specialist will work closely with the private client lawyer to identify and structure solutions that leverage the entire range of insurance products. You want a true independent here, not someone who receives incentives from a particular insurance company.

Other specialists in your network might include a credit expert to advise on loans; a corporate tax lawyer, especially for clients with fast-growing businesses; a derivatives specialist, who deals with concentrated tax positions; a securities lawyer, who supports the work of the derivatives specialist; an income tax specialist, for truly complex tax situations; an actuary, to support the work of the insurance specialist; and a valuation specialist, for appraising business interests, real estate or collectibles. There are, however, many other experts who may need to be part of your network, depending on the general needs of members of your target niche and the specific needs of your actual clients.

You don't necessarily need to establish a close relationship with every expert in your network. Instead, rely on your core team members—the private client lawyer and insurance specialist—to bring in their own experts as needed. But you do need to carefully select these two core team members. The members of your professional network must embody four key traits: specific expertise, integrity, professionalism and chemistry. Finding the right individuals will take some time and effort, so make sure you start this process early on. (Unfortunately, size constraints necessarily limit this book's discussion of selecting, vetting and managing your team of experts. CEG Worldwide's coaching programs, however,

Compensation for the Wealth Manager

As the wealth manager, the client is yours. You should therefore expect to receive a portion of each specialist's fee. (One clear exception is legal fees. In every case, your client hires the lawyer directly and you will receive no portion of his or her fees.)

Your compensation will vary according to the experts you're working with. Generally speaking, for insurance products, you can expect a fifty-fifty split of commissions (which are typically 90 percent to 120 percent of the first year's premium). For credit, you can expect a finder's fee or points. You should also get a portion of the commissions on derivatives transactions.

When you provide the client with investment management services yourself, you can (and should) charge a premium fee for these services, as compensation for providing all the other wealth management services. And when you execute strategies that have no products involved (for example, tax arbitrage between different countries), you can charge a project execution fee.

Obviously, all fees should be fully disclosed and transparent to your client. In addition, you should work with your compliance group to make sure you are properly licensed before moving forward.

Keeping the Network Running Well

Bringing together a group of top professionals is one thing; getting them to work together as a smoothly functioning and effective team is quite another. The following actions will help you get top performance from your network.

- **Establish a common vision.** You should be able not only to paint a picture for members of your network of what you all—together—are trying to accomplish, but also to achieve consensus around that vision. Your vision should include the comprehensive and client-centered wealth management you will provide, the satisfaction of working with other top-tier experts and the resulting financial rewards.
- **Agree on who's in charge.** The network will run smoothly only when members understand their roles. In particular, it must be clear that the clients are yours and that you are ultimately the one responsible for making decisions about what's best for them.
- **Formalize how and when members of the network will communicate.** Set up clear processes and timetables for meeting and collaborating. This is particularly important in a virtual network, where face-to-face contact is at a premium.

Continued on following page

include a detailed and systematic approach to locating and choosing experts.)

Uncovering Wealth Management Opportunities

Once your professional network is complete (or you at least have in place the two key players, the private client lawyer and the insurance specialist), you'll want to schedule a series of quarterly meetings. (Depending on the number of affluent clients you are working with, in some cases you may want to get together with your experts as frequently as monthly.) If your experts are located nearby, you should do these meetings in person, but telephone conferences work nearly as well after a business relationship is established. Set an agenda for each meeting and circulate it in advance.

At each meeting you'll present the overall situations of one to six of your clients by reviewing their Total Client Profiles. Your main goal for these meetings is to identify solutions to the challenges faced by your clients. An effective way to do this is to use a scenario-thinking process that identifies key issues, builds scenarios, identifies opportunities and then prioritizes those opportunities to address next steps in each client's four areas of advanced planning needs. When you come back to your client with recommended action in the Regular Progress Meetings, you may want to have the relevant expert available to join you in person or by phone to provide in-depth explanations.

Drawing on the information and insights you gained during the scenario-thinking process, you'll now clearly document the opportunities for actions that will address the client's needs. To do so, we recommend that you develop an advanced planning mind map. **Exhibit 4.9** provides an example of how such a mind map can be used to track the various activities involved in the four elements of advanced planning.

This mind map will contain recommended actions and document the order of priority of each action, as determined by you and the members of your network. It therefore allows the wealth manager and client to easily see the "big picture"—all activities are on a single page, and each is coded as to its status (already completed, in progress or slated for the future). Many advisors find that such mind maps are highly effective at guiding their work and focusing the discussion through each of the Regular Progress Meetings.

This chapter has covered a lot of ground. But once you've processed ten or 20 of your clients through the entire consultative process, you'll find that not only are you better at delivering wealth management than you ever imagined you would be, but also that your clients are more enthusiastic than ever about working with you. As a result, they'll be highly inclined to give you more of their assets to manage and to provide you with referrals. Let's now turn, then, to exactly how to grow your assets from existing clients and how to attract new ideal clients—and their assets.

- **Seek to continually improve your professional network meetings.** These sessions are when most group "bonding" will take place. Solicit feedback to help enhance your processes, facilitation skills and the recommendations you provide to clients.
- **Keep them motivated.** Finally, keep in mind the old adage that nothing succeeds like success. You'll keep the members of your professional network happy and motivated when they see the success of the team translated into income for them.

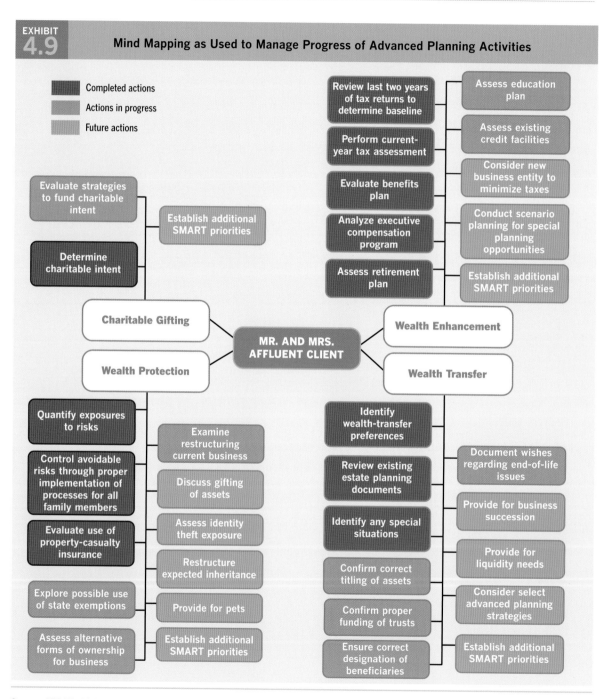

EXHIBIT 4.9

Mind Mapping as Used to Manage Progress of Advanced Planning Activities

Completed actions
Actions in progress
Future actions

Evaluate strategies to fund charitable intent

Establish additional SMART priorities

Determine charitable intent

Review last two years of tax returns to determine baseline

Assess education plan

Perform current-year tax assessment

Assess existing credit facilities

Evaluate benefits plan

Consider new business entity to minimize taxes

Analyze executive compensation program

Conduct scenario planning for special planning opportunities

Assess retirement plan

Establish additional SMART priorities

Charitable Gifting

Wealth Enhancement

MR. AND MRS. AFFLUENT CLIENT

Wealth Protection

Wealth Transfer

Quantify exposures to risks

Examine restructuring current business

Identify wealth-transfer preferences

Document wishes regarding end-of-life issues

Control avoidable risks through proper implementation of processes for all family members

Discuss gifting of assets

Review existing estate planning documents

Provide for business succession

Evaluate use of property-casualty insurance

Assess identity theft exposure

Identify any special situations

Provide for liquidity needs

Restructure expected inheritance

Confirm correct titling of assets

Consider select advanced planning strategies

Explore possible use of state exemptions

Provide for pets

Confirm proper funding of trusts

Assess alternative forms of ownership for business

Establish additional SMART priorities

Ensure correct designation of beneficiaries

Establish additional SMART priorities

Source: CEG Worldwide.

CHAPTER 5

Capture Assets and Acquire Clients

Capture Assets and Acquire Clients

With the right clients in hand and the right business model in place to serve them, it's time to focus on surefire business development processes that will bring you ever-increasing financial rewards. These are the three surest paths to growing your business:

- Capture additional assets from existing clients.
- Gather new ideal client referrals from existing clients.
- Form strategic alliances with attorneys and accountants.

In this chapter, we'll take a close look at each approach.

Capture Additional Assets from Existing Clients

You should use the consultative wealth management process not just with prospective clients, but with your existing clients as well. In fact, once you've determined which—if any—of your existing clients fit your ideal client profile, immediately implement the consultative process with them. Start with the Discovery Meeting (which, with existing clients, we call a "rediscovery" meeting).

Since they already trust you, working with these existing clients provides you with an ideal opportunity to refine your new consultative skills and process. Better served by your new wealth management orientation, these clients will be predisposed to give you more of their assets to manage and to refer prospective ideal clients to you.

We'll even go so far as to say that if you have a sufficient number of existing ideal clients, you shouldn't undertake *any* new business development efforts until you've completed at least ten rediscovery meetings. If you're like most advisors we've worked with, you'll find that your current clients represent a gold mine of additional business, there for the asking.

How can this be? While many advisors believe that most of their clients do not have other financial advisors, the data shows that this simply is not true, especially with respect to the affluent. Yes, most

(86.1 percent) clients with $500,000 to $1 million of investable assets have only one advisor, but for those with $1 million to $2 million of investable assets, only 26.4 percent have only one advisor, and for those with $2 million to $6 million of investable assets, only 2.5 percent have just a single advisor. (See **Exhibit 5.1**.)

Many wealthier individuals prefer to have their money invested with more than one advisor. In a sense, affluent people view having multiple advisors as a form of diversification. By spreading their money around, the wealthy feel that they can improve their overall investment returns, as well as the odds of finding at least one advisor who is really on top of things overall, someone who can reliably provide the services and solutions that they need and want.

There is considerable good news and (perhaps) some bad news here. If you have a compelling value proposition that sets you apart from other advisors—which your consultative wealth management process gives you—there's a good chance you can gain the business of prospective affluent ideal clients even when they already have other advisors.

Another piece of good news is that your existing affluent clients more than likely have assets in place with one or more other advisors (or simply sitting in a money market account, deposited in a CD or tucked under the proverbial mattress). The consultative process offers you numerous opportuni-

EXHIBIT 5.1	**Number of Financial Advisors**			
	Investable Assets			
Number of Advisors	**$500,000– $1 million**	**$1 million– $2 million**	**$2 million– $6 million**	**Total**
One	86.1%	26.4%	2.5%	42.1%
Two	12.6%	61.3%	56.0%	43.7%
Three or more	1.3%	12.3%	41.5%	14.2%

N = 1,417 affluent individuals.
Source: Russ Alan Prince and David A. Geracioti, *Cultivating the Middle-Class Millionaire*, 2005.

Capture Assets and Acquire Clients

ties to ask your affluent clients about such assets. Once you uncover these assets, you can offer a second opinion on how they are being managed. You can also simply ask your clients if they would like you to manage these other assets going forward. As you consistently delight and even thrill your clients with a top-notch client experience, they in turn will be inclined to offer you even more of their assets to manage.

More good news: You can ignore the many self-appointed industry gurus who say you should only work with clients when you have all their assets. This contention simply ignores the reality shown in Exhibit 5.1.

Now for the "bad" news—which really isn't all that bad if you see it as an opportunity. Whether you gain a new ideal client or are working with an existing one, that client, especially if he or she is very wealthy, is predisposed to placing some of his or her money with another advisor. And that's exactly why it's so important for you to differentiate yourself from other advisors through the consultative wealth management process.

One last piece of good news: Notwithstanding what **Exhibit 5.1** shows us, we believe that most clients, even the wealthiest ones, would prefer to have a *single* close relationship with a trusted financial advisor capable of meeting almost all their financial needs. Turn yourself into this trusted, capable advisor, and both additional assets and referrals will come your way from your affluent clients.

The Process for (and Secret to) Capturing More Assets

It's far easier to grow your business by gathering additional assets from existing clients than by the expensive, time-consuming route of prospecting for new clients. But there's a secret to captur-

Critical Success Factors for Asset Capture

Many advisors feel uncomfortable asking for additional assets. Keeping these important points in mind will make it easier:

- When you deliver a consistent, top-notch (WOW) level of service and rely on a systematic consultative process, your clients are likely to be increasingly satisfied with you and have good reason to give you more assets.
- As a result of your Discovery Meetings, you'll already know what other assets your clients have. You'll be able to specify exactly what you're asking for and why.
- Ask for additional assets when your clients are most satisfied with you, for example, during your Regular Progress Meetings or after you've successfully provided an advanced planning solution.
- Although it's theoretically possible that a client might be offended or otherwise put off by your asking for more assets, we've never heard of it happening.

ing additional assets from existing clients, one that's a key part of our proven five-step process:

Step 1. Set Expectations

Keeping in mind that each of your affluent clients probably has multiple advisors, your goal is to increase your share of your clients' assets by ensuring that they are completely satisfied with their relationship with you. Set expectations by reminding your clients at each of your Regular Progress Meetings that you are keenly interested in their overall well-being, which includes taking into account their overall asset allocation and the ways that any assets not placed with you are being managed.

Step 2. Review the Client Relationship

Periodically inquire as to what your clients do and do not like about their relationship with you. In addition to asking about this at your Regular Progress Meetings, conduct an annual client satisfaction survey. Remember, investment performance, which you can't completely control in any case, only goes so far in guaranteeing client satisfaction. What you *can* fully control is the quality of your client relationships and of the services you deliver. If a client is blasé about your relationship, only exceptional investment performance will garner additional assets. But if your relationship is exceptionally strong—something the consultative process facilitates—you are likely to gain additional assets even without exceptional investment performance.

Step 3. Identify Asset Transfer Opportunities

You must have a clear understanding of the overall assets of your clients—what they have and who's managing it. The consultative process provides you with this knowledge. Once you've completed a

EXHIBIT 5.2	Clients Who Were Asked for More Assets

Percentage of each surveyed advisor's top 50 clients who were asked for more assets by the advisor

Clients Asked	
None	51.1%
1%–24% of clients	18.4%
25%–49% of clients	18.2%
50%–75% of clients	11.9%
More than 75% of clients	0.0%

N = 1,097 advisors.

Source: AIM/Gresham, *Wealth Management 2000*.

Analysis: CEG Worldwide.

Discovery (or rediscovery) Meeting, you'll know about the assets managed by other advisors and be able to target them for capture.

Step 4. Ask for Additional Assets

On occasion a very satisfied client may offer you additional assets without prompting. For the most part, however, you must ask for the additional assets.

Step 5. Thank Your Clients

Let your clients know that you appreciate the trust they've placed in you, whether or not you have received any additional assets. Always keep in mind that your relationships with your affluent clients are the ultimate key to your long-term success.

What, then, is the secret to additional asset capture? It's Step 4: You actually have to ask. As **Exhibit 5.2** shows, more than half of 1,097 surveyed advisors did not ask a single client for additional assets in the previous year. No advisor asked more than 75 percent of their clients. It's simple: If you don't ask, you won't get—so go ahead and ask.

EXHIBIT 5.7	Gross Revenue per CPA Firm from Financial Services	
Rating of Advisor	**Percentage**	**Consequences**
Excellent	26.7%	■ Will refer others ■ Will add assets
Fair	69.7%	■ Receptive to other advisors ■ Will not add assets
Poor	3.6%	■ Will switch their advisors soon

Source: Russ Alan Prince and Brett Van Bortel, *The Millionaire's Advisor*™, 2003.
Analysis: CEG Worldwide.

Formalize Your Client Referrals Program

As **Exhibit 5.3** shows, only slightly more than one-quarter (26.7 percent) of affluent clients rated their advisors as "excellent," while the remaining nearly three-quarters (73.3 percent) rated their advisors as "fair" or "poor." It's clear that the opportunity for business growth through referrals is very significant because clients are generally not very satisfied with the advisors they already have.

Put yourself in the shoes of an affluent individual who, like the great majority of affluent clients, finds his or her financial advisor to be only of "fair" quality. Such a person is likely to be receptive to working with other advisors. In fact, nearly three out of four are likely to switch to another advisor if they find the right one. This is why it's so very important for you to be in the "excellent" category—part of the "switched to" rather than the "switched away from" camp. You will ensure this by providing a consistent and superlative client experience.

Not only are satisfied clients more likely to stay with you, they are more likely to provide referrals. They want to share their great experience of working with you with their friends and business associates (just like you want to tell people about the great book you just read or great massage therapist you just found).

Our research shows the clear link between client satisfaction and client inclination to provide referrals. As **Exhibit 5.4** illustrates, satisfied clients provided, on average, 2.1 referrals in the previous year. Not surprisingly, as client satisfaction increases, so does the number of referrals. For highly satisfied or loyal clients, the figure is significantly higher—11.8 referrals, on average, over the previous 12 months. Such a referral rate can lead to exceptional growth for your business and may be the only type of growth you need to cultivate.

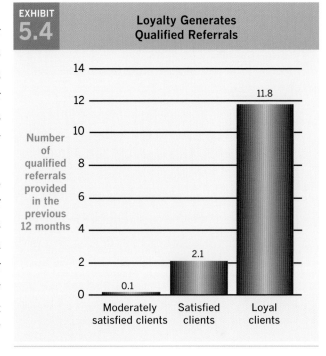

EXHIBIT 5.4

Loyalty Generates Qualified Referrals

Number of qualified referrals provided in the previous 12 months

N = 1,417 affluent individuals.
Source: Russ Alan Prince and David A. Geracioti, *Cultivating the Middle-Class Millionaire*, 2005.

The 12-Step Client Referral Request Process

Don't make the mistake of waiting for your clients to give you referrals. While a highly satisfied client may from time to time give you a referral without being prompted, you can't count on a steady stream of such referrals. Just as you have to ask your clients for additional assets, you'll have to ask them for ideal client referrals—again and again.

Begin to ask for ideal client referrals when prospects first become clients. This means asking during the Mutual Commitment Meeting, then at the 45-Day Follow-up Meeting and continuing at every Regular Progress Meeting. We recommend the following 12-step process:

Step 1. Set the Stage to Ask

Many advisors are uncomfortable asking for referrals, because they feel that they are asking their clients to do something that does not benefit the clients. You can overcome any such reluctance by properly setting expectations right from the beginning. Explain to your clients exactly why it is in their own interest to provide you with referrals.

Let them know that the time you spend marketing detracts from the time you have to focus on them. By saving you a great deal of marketing effort, your clients are literally helping you to help them.

To the extent you provide your clients a great experience—truly "WOW" them—they are likely to want to share that same experience with their friends and business associates, both for the sheer joy of sharing something valuable and for the acknowledgment that comes from helping make someone else's life better.

Step 2. Ask for the Referral

Now pose the referral request question. Simply state exactly your ideal client profile and ask if they know anyone who fits the bill: "As you know, we work primarily with successful aesthetic dentists, such as yourself. Do you know any other successful aesthetic dentists in our area who might benefit from our services as you have?"

Step 3. Ask for Additional Referrals

Once you've received a name, ask for another. Just say this: "Great! Who else comes to mind?" Continue to ask until the client has no more names to offer. A reasonable expectation is three to five, but why be reasonable?

Step 4. Gather Contact Information

Once you have a list of names, ask for background and contact information as well as the best way to approach each. Do this after the clients have given you names. Do not interrupt the momentum while they are giving you names.

Step 5. Ask for a Personal Introduction

Ask each client to provide a "heads-up" to each of the referrals to expect your call. As you move farther upmarket, personal introductions become even more important and more expected. Also, given the complexity of "do not call" regulations and the prevalence of assistants screening calls at work, a personal introduction is certainly the most desirable introduction to a qualified prospect.

Step 6. Commit to Follow Up

Assure your clients that you will follow up on all referrals that they make. In those cases where they are not providing you with a personal introduction, let them know that you will follow up on your own.

Common Mistakes in the Referral Process

Here are a few common referral process mistakes that you can easily avoid:

- **Failing to ask.** As with capturing additional assets, if you don't ask, you don't get. So go ahead and ask. The worst that can happen is that your client says "no."
- **Making yourself seem too busy.** Many of us try to make ourselves look successful by appearing to be very busy. Don't give this impression. If you do, your clients won't want to add to your burden by referring someone else to you.
- **Failing to follow through.** Follow through religiously on every referral. Otherwise you not only waste your time and effort, you lose credibility with the referring client. (Imagine how embarrassed your client will be if he or she mentions you to the referral and finds out you never made contact.)
- **Failing to stick with your ideal client profile.** Don't blindly pursue every referral that comes your way. If the occasional prospect who doesn't precisely match your ideal client profile happens to have significant investable assets and you know you could easily add substantial value to him or her, it might make sense to take this individual as a client. But this is a judgment call. Remember that, for the most part, the more you are distracted from your core competencies, the less successful you're going to be.

Step 7. Wrap Up the Meeting

As you wrap up the meeting, express your appreciation and remind clients that by helping you save time on marketing, they are helping you to be able to spend more time serving them. It's also important to clearly delineate your goals. You can say something like "I now have 32 ideal clients. In order to stay extremely focused on serving my clients well, I'm going to accept only 100 clients. The sooner I can get there, the sooner I can stop spending time on acquiring new clients."

Step 8. Thank Each Client

Express your thanks in a handwritten note. This has become a lost art and is greatly appreciated. If you don't have good handwriting, then print. Failing that, you can send an email, but this is much less effective. Your personal handwritten note should ideally be sent out on the same day that you receive the referral, and no later than the following day.

Step 9. Call Each Prospect

Your goal for the initial contact with each referral prospect should be to arrange a Discovery Meeting. The person will respond in one of three ways, each of which requires a different response from you.

1. **"No."** Prospects who decline to meet will typically do so because they already have a financial advisor. If this is the case, then inquire as to whether they would like a free second opinion on their portfolio.
2. **"Maybe."** You will seldom get this response, but when you do, it's most often because the prospect has hesitation about cost. If so, let the prospect know that there's no cost for an initial Discovery Meeting and that in any case you wouldn't take him or her on as a client unless you were sure you could add real value.
3. **"Yes."** Schedule a date and time to get together. Explain that you will send a follow-up letter outlining the financial information and records you would like to have him or her bring to the meeting in order to make the meeting extremely productive.

Step 10. Send an Invitation to the Prospect

Immediately after arranging the Discovery Meeting, send a follow-up letter to prepare him or her for the meeting, as we discussed in Chapter 4.

Step 11. Let Each Client Know the Results

Referral sources are curious about how things work out, so it's important that you inform them about what happened (while being conscious of client confidentiality, of course). A quick note or an email is better than a phone call, but immediate feedback is desirable either way. Lack of feedback devalues your clients' efforts on your behalf and can damage your all-important client-advisor relationships.

Step 12. Thank Each Client—Again

Once clients make referrals they are likely to refer again. Keep your referral sources inclined to make additional referrals by acknowledging how much you appreciate their assistance, which allows you to focus the vast majority of your time on solving your clients' financial challenges, rather than marketing.

Some advisors like to thank their referral sources with small gifts, such as gift baskets. Other advisors like to take the client out to dinner, but we've found (not surprisingly) that most clients prefer dinner with their spouses to dinner with their financial advisors. This makes a gift certificate to a client's favorite restaurant a nice gift. Be sure to be aware of current regulatory limits on the annual total allowable value of gifts. Whether or not you give your client a gift, and whether or not the prospect works out, it's important that you acknowledge your clients for providing referrals.

Form Strategic Alliances with Attorneys and Accountants

Developing strategic alliances with other professionals who are in a position to refer ideal prospective clients to you is a great way to boost your long-term business growth. Consider that affluent individuals *want* to find their financial advisors through such referrals. As **Exhibit 5.5** shows, 54.2 percent of the affluent clients surveyed reported that a referral from an accountant or an attorney was an important way to find their primary financial advisors.

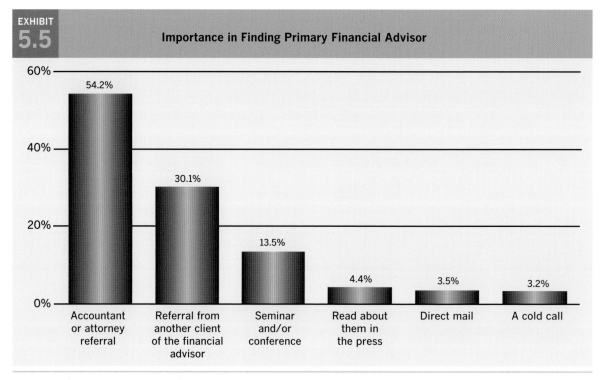

EXHIBIT 5.5

Importance in Finding Primary Financial Advisor

- Accountant or attorney referral: 54.2%
- Referral from another client of the financial advisor: 30.1%
- Seminar and/or conference: 13.5%
- Read about them in the press: 4.4%
- Direct mail: 3.5%
- A cold call: 3.2%

N = 1,417 affluent individuals.
Source: Russ Alan Prince and David A. Geracioti, *Cultivating the Middle-Class Millionaire*, 2005.

What exactly is a strategic alliance? In contrast to informal referral arrangements, a strategic alliance is an agreement that creates a vested interest in each partner to help the other grow. This agreement creates the "economic glue" that holds together a mutually beneficial partnership. The agreement is a formalized ongoing relationship that has been clearly spelled out and committed to by both sides and sets the stage for a long-term profitable relationship for both parties. At the heart of the agreement is a set of genuine benefits to the other professional, which results in additional revenue to the other firm.

It's important to not confuse strategic alliances with your professional network of financial experts, as described in Chapter 4. A strategic alliance is a business development relationship, where each party enters into the alliance with the clear expectation that it will lead to additional business. The professional network serves a different purpose: to enable you to meet your affluent clients' wealth management needs. In some cases an expert in your network may also provide referrals (for example, your private client attorney), but it's best to keep the development of strategic alliances as a separate focus until you have firmly established your expert team.

While the detailed process of how to establish strategic alliances is beyond the scope of this book (and covered in detail in our coaching programs), they are so potentially valuable that we believe it's worthwhile to describe the economic rationale behind them and to provide a brief overview of the alliance-creation process. When you understand the potential value of strategic alliances, we're confident that you'll do what it takes to create them.

Strategic Alliances with CPAs

CPAs are extremely attractive strategic partners for financial advisors for at least four reasons:

1. CPAs are often their clients' most trusted advisors.
2. Their clients wish to obtain financial products from them.
3. Financial services offer substantial revenue opportunities both for CPAs and the financial advisors they work with.
4. Many CPAs are highly motivated to offer their clients financial services, for a variety of reasons.

To start, almost all surveys of affluent individuals show CPAs to be the most trusted professional advisors. By creating strategic alliances with CPAs, advisors can benefit from this built-in trust.

Because the affluent trust their CPAs, they are keenly interested in obtaining financial products from them. As **Exhibit 5.6** shows, 52.6 percent of individuals are interested in getting investment products from their accountants. Even more (68.8 percent) would like their accountants to provide insurance products as well.

As for the economic opportunity, when financial advisors and CPAs successfully execute strategic

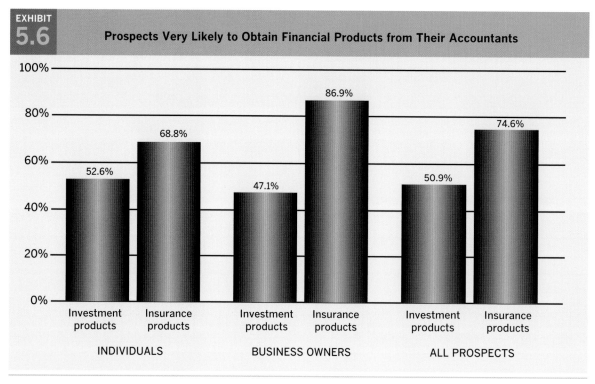

EXHIBIT 5.6

Prospects Very Likely to Obtain Financial Products from Their Accountants

N = 1,521 individuals and 719 business owners.
Source: Russ Alan Prince, *Accountants as Wealth Managers*, 2003.

alliances, there is the potential for substantial revenue generation for both sides. **Exhibit 5.7** shows the results from a nationwide study of 394 CPA firms already offering financial services in some way. Across the board, we found that CPA firms that leveraged strategic alliances with financial advisors earned substantially more revenue than those firms with in-house financial services and had a much higher profit margin while doing so, since they did not have the direct costs and overhead associated with having employees. (The first two rows of revenue figures in **Exhibit 5.7** show the *gross* revenue of the firms offering financial services in-house. The third and fourth rows, showing accounting firms

EXHIBIT 5.7	Gross Revenue per CPA Firm from Financial Services		
	2003 Revenue (Average)	**2004 Projected Revenue (Average)**	**Projected Increase from 2003 to 2004**
Smaller firms with in-house financial services	$392,000	$546,000	39.3%
Larger firms with in-house financial services	$718,000	$1,037,000	44.4%
Smaller firms using outside financial services providers	$834,000	$1,359,000	62.9%
Larger firms using outside financial services providers	$1,241,000	$2,451,000	97.5%

N = 394 CPA firms.
Source: CEG Worldwide, *Capturing the Opportunity*, 2004.

making use of outside strategic alliances, are *net* revenue numbers representing these firms' portion of the overall revenue generated.) We defined smaller firms as those with three or fewer accounting partners; those with four or more partners were considered larger firms.

Notably, CPAs don't want to enter the financial services market just to earn more revenue. As **Exhibit 5.8** shows, 93.4 percent of CPA firms who were surveyed gave "to better serve clients" as their first reason for entering the financial services markets, 86.0 percent said it was to be more profitable, 62.2 percent said it was to counter pressures on their accounting practices, and 60.7 percent said it was to keep up with other CPA firms that were providing financial services.

The advisors in our coaching programs who have built strategic alliances with CPAs are experiencing the highest growth of any advisors we work with. The process begins by determining the most suitable potential partners and then narrowing it down to the top five candidates, using criteria such as how highly respected the firm is, the firm's overall philosophy and whether the firm is open to working with other professional advisors. Next, you'll want to arrange a meeting with a senior partner

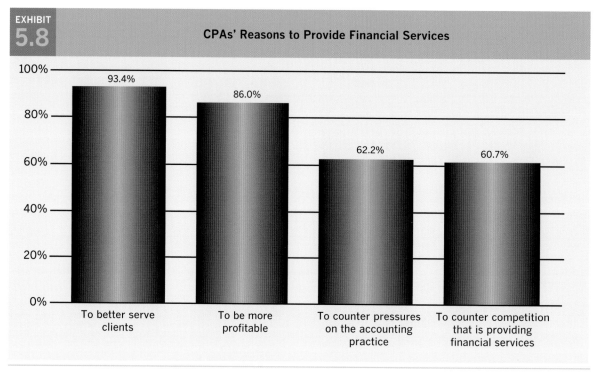

EXHIBIT 5.8

CPAs' Reasons to Provide Financial Services

N = 394 CPA firms.
Source: CEG Worldwide, *Capturing the Potential*, 2004.

at the firm and explore the possibility of creating a working relationship. After arranging a meeting, send a follow-up letter to confirm the date and time and to reiterate your goals for the meeting.

At the meeting, interview the senior partner to determine whether the CPA firm would be an appropriate strategic alliance partner for you. You can share industry research to show how valuable it can be to the CPA firm to have a relationship in place with an advisor like yourself. Before the meeting is over you should be able to make a decision about whether you want to work with the firm. If so, you can begin to identify opportunities to work together through further brainstorming meetings with key members of the firm and then create an action plan for the strategic alliance. You'll then set up a meeting to present the action plan, which should lead to a commitment from all important stakeholders, including the CPA firm's managing partner. As soon as you achieve consensus on the plan, execute it. It's important to achieve some success early on so that all stakeholders remain committed to the plan and achieving its goals.

Strategic Alliances with Attorneys

The opportunities to grow your business by building strategic alliances do not end with CPAs. Another type of professional advisor—private client lawyers—have deep relationships in place with their clients. By forming strategic alliances with these attorneys, you'll gain access to their clients at the times when they most need your assistance. Most significantly, you'll position yourself to receive referrals for clients who have just received inheritances or are in the process of restructuring key aspects of their financial lives.

> **Ingredients for a Successful Alliance with a CPA**
>
> **Economic glue.** Do not form a strategic alliance unless there is a revenue share that creates "economic glue." We have simply found that without this economic glue, parties drift quickly apart, or worse, the CPA firm will decide to offer financial services without you.
>
> **Help from compliance.** Remember to work with your compliance department to make sure any agreement is properly drafted. It is important to note that accountants will need to be licensed.
>
> **No shortcuts.** Don't attempt workarounds such as renting space or paying for the CPA firm's review of an investment plan. Don't work with anyone who's willing to cut corners. You're in this for the long haul—do it right.

The strategic alliances you'll develop with these attorneys are quite specific. You'll provide the expertise the attorneys need to enhance and build their businesses. In exchange, the attorneys will provide you with qualified affluent client referrals.

A successful strategic alliance with an attorney has several very attractive features:

- The attorney refers affluent clients to you on a regular basis. You will receive a steady stream of prequalified affluent clients for whom you can add significant value.
- You are the primary financial advisor to whom the attorney makes referrals. You will be first in the mind of the attorney when it comes to referrals. As a result, you will receive all or most of the attorney's referrals.

■ The attorney is actively looking to make referrals to you. The attorney is motivated to make referrals to you and thus is always keeping an eye out for clients who are suitable for referral.

Strategic alliances with attorneys are in some respects similar to those with accountants. In other ways they are quite different, as shown in overview form in **Exhibit 5.9**.

As we mentioned, the type of attorney that offers the best prospects for a profitable strategic alliance is the private client lawyer. These attorneys already routinely make referrals for their wealthy clients to obtain the investment services they need. More often than not, those referrals result in business for the referred advisor. According to a study of 619 private client lawyers, an average of 10 percent of these attorneys are already referring their clients to investment professionals, and the average amount of investable assets per client referred was $2.7 million. The study also found that nearly three-quarters (73.2 percent) of clients used the financial advisors referred by their attorneys.

The study also showed that many private client lawyers—24.7 percent of those surveyed—are actively looking for eligible clients to refer. Perhaps best of all, the referral potential for financial advisors appears to remain largely untapped. Three out of four of the lawyers surveyed had not been approached by a single investment professional in the previous year. This spells opportunity for those financial advisors who do take the initiative in contacting private client lawyers.

The process for forming strategic alliances with attorneys is similar to the one you will use for creating strategic alliances with CPA firms. After determining the most suitable potential partners and then narrowing it down to the top five candidates, make an initial call to explore a working relationship. Once you've set up a meeting, interview the attorney in depth about his or her business, phi-

Real-World Success Story: Forging Strategic Alliances

Gordon Owens, a senior vice president of investments with Robert W. Baird Co.'s private asset management group in Orlando, Florida, has seen a dramatic turnaround in his efforts to build strategic alliances—which Owens says had been "an utter disaster."

Armed with a new approach to delivering exceptional client service, a step-by-step process for building winning alliances with professionals, and supported by CEG Worldwide's proprietary research, Owens quickly found himself breaking through the barriers that had stymied him for years. "I now have the support and capabilities that prove to accountants and lawyers that I'll take exceptional care of their clients," says Owens. "As a result, I've built two strategic alliances since February—one with a lawyer and one with a CPA—compared to none during the past 12 years. I'd call that quite an improvement!"

	EXHIBIT 5.9	Contrasting Strategic Alliances with Accountants and Attorneys
Attribute	**Strategic Alliances with Accountants**	**Strategic Alliances with Attorneys**
Economic glue	Typically takes the form of a revenue share.	Typically takes the form of indirect financial incentives, such as methods for enhancing the partner's business, in exchange for referrals.
Level of formality	Very formal.	Informal.
Point of contact	While initial contact is with a single partner, the alliance must gain the backing of all major firm partners.	Alliance is generally made one-on-one with a single member of the firm; other partners are not involved.
Type of accountant/ attorney	Alliances may be with accountants in a range of specialties.	Alliances are primarily restricted to private client lawyers.

Source: CEG Worldwide.

losophy and openness to working with someone like yourself. You'll also share industry research and explain the value that you can provide. If both you and the attorney decide it makes sense to go forward, you'll identify opportunities to work together, draw up your recommendations and present them. Once you get agreement from the attorney, jump into implementing the recommendations to ensure the early successes that leave both parties feeling good and deeply engaged.

There's no doubt that there are significant opportunities out there for advisors to form strategic alliances with private client lawyers. Ultimately, these alliances—like alliances with CPAs—represent a triple win that benefits the referring professional; the financial advisor; and, most important, the client. If you're endeavoring to manage your practice as a business, the subject we'll turn to next, it certainly makes good sense to consider initiating such strategic relationships while you stay focused on capturing additional assets and gaining referrals from existing clients.

CHAPTER 6

Manage Your Practice as a Business

Manage Your Practice as a Business

We are part of a great industry, one that most of us joined in order to be great financial advisors helping clients achieve their most important dreams. Part of being a great advisor is recognizing that we must also be great entrepreneurs— entrepreneurs who happen to have chosen the financial services industry.

There's a huge difference here. Your decision to become a great financial advisor, or to become a great entrepreneur who is also a financial advisor, will determine not only how profitable you are, but also how much impact you have on your clients.

To become a great entrepreneur, you must learn to say "no" and to embrace the reality that you can't work with everyone who comes along. Instead, as we discussed in Chapter 3, you must only take on those clients who are right for you. With these ideal clients in place, you can focus on creating systems and processes that enable you to profitably and consistently deliver an experience that absolutely thrills and delights your clients.

In essence, you will build world-class systems to provide highly customized services for your ideal clients—services that are right on the money and that reliably meet or exceed their expectations. We believe that it's not only possible but downright necessary for you to leverage your efforts in a systematic manner.

Consider the first meeting with a prospective client. Advisors who are primarily focused on being great advisors might spend a lot of time describing the intricacies of their "unique" investment solutions and how those solutions can maximize the probability of the client achieving his or her goals. But advisors who are determined to become great entrepreneurs will have highly refined processes in place—such as the carefully planned Discovery Meeting and Total Client Profile processes we described in Chapter 4—that are highly efficient and tightly focused on the client. In the long run, these processes will deliver a consistently superior client experience as they help ideal clients more effectively achieve their goals.

Similarly, while an advisor might be able to design advanced planning solutions in a one-off fashion, the entrepreneur is ensured of arriving at the optimal advanced planning solutions for each client through the well-managed expert network process that he or she has put in place.

Great entrepreneurship for financial advisors boils down to clarity of purpose (identifying and serving the right clients), focus (creating a compelling value proposition) and execution (systematically delivering the client experience promised by your value proposition). You also must have the support mechanisms that will enable you to do what you love—profitably helping clients achieve their financial goals—over and over again, in a way that does not consume your entire life. (Many advisors are in this business because they love helping others. Ironically, when these advisors fail to run their businesses well, they are the ones who often become overwhelmed.)

Your goal is to build a simple, elegant business that runs systematically and almost automatically grows in value over time. To create such a great business, you must have the absolute clarity and focused execution needed to achieve your vision. In short, you have to manage your practice as a business. In this chapter we'll cover four critical ways of doing this:

- ◼ Create a compelling vision and business plan.
- ◼ Use technology wisely.
- ◼ Blueprint your systems and processes.
- ◼ Deliver "WOW" service.

Create a Compelling Vision and Business Plan

To be successful on purpose, you need to be 100 percent clear about what you're doing. Not only will this clarity boost your own performance, it will motivate and unify your staff, business partners, other stakeholders and even your clients. A clear vision is an emotional lighthouse that will continuously pull you and your team toward your objectives. As Stephen Covey eloquently put it, to maximize the likelihood of success, you must "begin with the end in mind."

By clearly defining your vision, you'll know precisely where you want to take your business and be able to accurately judge whether you're heading in the right direction. Many studies have shown that when business leaders effectively communicate a compelling vision of the future, their constituents report significantly higher levels of these success factors:

- Job satisfaction
- Commitment and loyalty
- Esprit de corps
- Clarity about organizational values
- Organizational pride
- Organizational productivity
- Retention of clients and staff

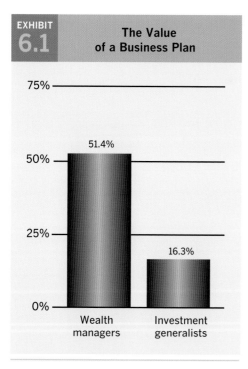

EXHIBIT
6.1
**The Value
of a Business Plan**

75%

51.4%

50%

25%

16.3%

0%

Wealth
managers

Investment
generalists

N = 2,094 financial advisors.
Source: CEG Worldwide, 2007.

Make sure your vision consists of bite-size pieces—manageable portions. You'll be able to more easily communicate these smaller pieces to your stakeholders, construct a business plan from them and be able to execute them to achieve early wins. When the going occasionally gets tough—as it does for everyone—the clarity of your vision and business plan will determine whether you and your staff are overwhelmed or remain enthusiastic and tenaciously effective. With a clear vision, you'll find yourself jumping out of bed each morning, raring to get going.

The following vision-creation process has proven very useful to advisors in our coaching programs:

Step 1. Create

Start by creating a compelling vision of success—an exciting picture of what your business will look like three years from now when you have successfully built a world-class wealth management practice or firm. Take some time to ask yourself *why* you're in the business, *what* you are hoping to achieve and *how* you will make it happen. You are a unique individual, and your vision must uniquely represent who you are, what's important to you, and how through your own hard work and determination you'll make it all happen.

Step 2. Communicate

To have maximum impact, you must communicate your vision effectively to your business partners, clients and other constituents. To motivate people, communicate your vision in a clear, lively manner. Describe it in a simple and direct way that moves and touches people. The word "inspire" means "to breathe life into." Leaders breathe life into their visions by the skill with which they communicate them. Use metaphors; analogies; examples; anecdotes and powerful images; and a positive, expressive communication style to bring your vision to life for others.

Step 3. Act

Most important, you must act to make the future you envision a reality. As futurist Joel Barker said,

> **"Vision without action is merely a dream.**
> **Action without vision just passes the time.**
> **Vision with action can change the world."**

Once you have created your compelling vision and have tested it out on a few people inside and outside of your office, begin to act by constructing a thoughtful business plan around it. Successful people are intentional and do things on purpose. Activity alone is not enough—value is derived only from deliberate action. A well-crafted business plan can ensure that your actions are intentional and focused on clear aims. Plan for success and you will dramatically increase the odds of realizing that success.

As **Exhibit 6.1** shows, advisors who are high-earning wealth managers are more than three times as likely to have a business plan than are advisors who are investment generalists. And while only 51.4 percent of the wealth managers have a business plan, we have no doubt that those without a plan would experience an even greater level of success if they took the time to create one.

For most advisors a traditional, formal business plan is unnecessary. Instead, we recommend a streamlined plan that is designed for the 21st century. It should consist of these three parts:

1. A PowerPoint presentation describing you and your business
2. A spreadsheet of key financial projections
3. An executive summary

The **PowerPoint presentation** should address eight key areas, as described in the sidebar. Once you have these elements in place, move on to your **financial projections.** Properly constructed, financial projections will concisely communicate the essence of your business in an easy-to-understand way. To ensure that your projections are accurate, enlist a financial expert to help you put them together or, at a minimum, to review what you've already done. The quickest way to lose credibility with your team or with outside investors is to have them point out obvious problems with your numbers. Make sure your projections are as up to date as possible and that you can explain the rationale behind every number.

Finally, write an **executive summary** (which will actually come first in the plan) that highlights the most important parts of your plan. It should be no longer than three pages and should succinctly answer these four questions:

1. **What do you do?** Provide a brief description of your business, value proposition, business model and how you make money.
2. **Why should readers care about what you do?** Tell the readers what's in it for them. How can they benefit from the plans you have for your business?
3. **Who are you?** Outline your background, education and unique qualifications.
4. **What are the key numbers readers should care about?** Include current revenue, net income and your forecasts for how these will increase.

As you put together the elements of your business plan, keep two key goals in mind. First, you want to communicate your vision effectively—a business plan without a vision will simply not work. Second, you want the plan to describe how you will deliver to your clients the "WOW" service that will win their hearts and minds.

Use Technology Wisely

When it comes to technology, we live in the best of times and the worst of times. On the one hand, technology today is more useful and—dare we say it—cooler than ever before. Even more than that, the pace at which new and useful technology is introduced is constantly accelerating.

On the other hand, no matter how cool or useful your technology is, it will help you grow your business only when it frees you up to do what's really important. Both research and our experience consistently show that the most successful advisors spend the lion's share of their time on two key activities:

- Client relationship management
- Business development

This bears repeating: Technology is valuable only when it enables you to spend time on these key activities. If you don't use technology wisely, you'll waste enormous amounts of time on activities that seem relevant and useful (answering emails, playing phone tag, surfing the Web) but actually amount to significant time drains.

The best advisors keep abreast of new technological developments but only adopt or upgrade technology when it supports their relationship management or business development tasks. Here are the four areas of technology that you should keep on top of:

1. **Client-related tools.** These are tools that your clients come directly into contact with, including email, your Web site and an email newsletter.

The Key Elements of a 21st-Century Business Plan

1. **The Market Opportunity**
- Discussion of the affluent market, the needs of affluent clients and the misalignment of most financial service providers with the affluent market
- Opportunities in your specific market niche(s)
- Confirmation of the opportunity based on business experience to date

2. **Your Compelling Value Proposition**
- How you help clients make smart decisions and avoid costly mistakes with their money (for example, by using the CCM Process)
- Your expertise within your market niche
- If applicable, your partner's (or partners') expertise within your market niche(s)
- Why wealthy individuals will want to work with you

3. **Your Unique Qualifications**
- What you bring to the table (for example, rainmaking skills, expertise within your market niche, existing client relationships, credibility marketing ability)
- What your team brings to the table
- What your partners (if any) bring to the table

Continued on following page

4. Your Business Model

- Discussion of your wealth management business model
- Your service delivery methodology (for example, the CCM Process and all other key systems and processes)
- How your business model differs from that of your competition

5. Leveragability of Your Business Model

- Clear explanation of how you will scale your business

6. How You Will Make Money

- How you have made money in the past
- How you currently make money
- How you will maintain or increase your profit margin as you grow

7. Risk Factors

- Your specific risk factors (for example, reliance on key personnel including yourself, limited resources, financial market uncertainties and regulatory changes)
- What could go wrong

8. How You Will Use Any Funds You Raise (if appropriate)

- Specifically how you will use investors' money effectively to increase revenue and profit

2. **Productivity-related tools.** These technologies are designed to enhance your efficiency and productivity. Under this category comes an efficient phone system; a good client relationship management software program (a must-have, because nothing is more valuable than your client relationships); a digital voice recorder; other standard office productivity programs and utilities for word processing, graphics generation, document backup and storage, voice recognition, document management and collaboration, Web conferencing, and presentation and training; virtual assistants; and wireless access to the Web (through a device such as a BlackBerry or iPhone).

3. **Technical support tools.** These provide all your financial services solutions and include client profiling and research tools, your back-office platform (typically through your broker-dealer or custodian), portfolio management and reporting software, financial planning software, online compliance support (if you don't have access to a compliance officer), and stock-option planning software.

4. **Time management tools.** These are processes and technologies that help you get the most from your limited time. You must deal efficiently with emails, voice mails and phone calls, which otherwise can be hugely distracting. It's also important to run effective—and whenever possible, brief—meetings, and to set an overall open-door management style that still lets you have your door closed most of the time. Random interruptions and socializing will simply kill your overall productivity.

With so many technologies available, you must choose your tools carefully and then use them effectively—without getting in over your head. Here are four simple rules for maximizing your use of technology:

1. **Stay slightly behind the leading edge.** Keep current, but stay away from the "bleeding edge"— you don't need to be a first adopter of any new technology.

2. **Don't develop new technology on your own (even if you can) or pay someone to develop new technology for you.** There's almost always an off-the-shelf solution that will do whatever you need to have done.

3. **Regularly assess your use of technology.** Ask yourself whether the technology you use actually enhances your productivity and frees you up for your core competencies and activities. Pay attention to what other top advisors you know are doing so that you don't fall too far behind in any key area.

4. **Rely on the advice of true experts.** To keep your time free for your most important activities, turn to trusted technology providers for help. For example, if your telephone and voice-mail system is out of date, don't spend time researching options. Find a professional who can rapidly present you with solid recommendations and then take the work all the way through to conclusion. Also, when implementing new software programs, take advantage of training programs offered by the vendor. Experts estimate that we only use 20 percent of the capabilities of most software programs. Make sure your staff members are true experts and that you are getting maximum return on your investment through in-depth training on key software programs.

Careful technology choices will certainly support your relationship management and business development efforts, but don't for one minute think that technology will create a profitable-on-purpose business where there wasn't one before. Technology is a tool—use it wisely or it will end up using you.

Blueprint Systems and Processes

Successful entrepreneurs excel at creating compelling visions for their businesses. Working from their visions, they build the systems and processes they need and that will create a meaningful competitive advantage by differentiating themselves from their competitors in their customers' eyes.

Often, however, these systems and processes exist only in the mind of the entrepreneur or a key staff person and are not documented. This causes two problems. First, the systems never become a clear reality for anyone else in the firm. Second, because the systems exist only in someone's mind, they are impossible to maintain in the absence of that person.

By establishing repeatable systems and processes, you create a defined experience—both externally (for clients and prospects) and internally (for staff)—for everyone who comes into contact with the business. And when you document, or blueprint, those processes, the documentation itself increases the strategic value of your business. You'll have a turnkey operation that almost anyone could run, even if you're no longer part of the firm.

In short, you need to create and blueprint both systems and processes that deliver great results without relying on extraordinary personal intervention by you or your staff. This is the only way to ensure consistent, outstanding experiences for both your affluent clients and your team members, whether you're there or not. And it's the only way to assure potential strategic buyers, either now or in the future, that your firm's successful operation is not solely dependent on your presence.

There are two major categories of systems and processes that you should build, master and blueprint for your business. The first consists of your **client experience systems**, which act outside of the firm and are dedicated to acquiring, servicing and communicating with affluent clients. The second major category is made up of your **business systems**. These internal systems are responsible for efficient management, profit generation and equity creation.

Every system and process should be precisely defined, perfected and blueprinted. Don't try to do all this blueprinting by yourself to the detriment of your most important activities—managing client relationships and business development. Instead, assign one or more key staff members to undertake the blueprinting process in a reasonable time frame with your guidance and assistance.

When the blueprinting is complete, make sure that everyone in your organization has access to all the blueprints. Invite them to comment on and improve them. Your staff members—who actually carry out the majority of the blueprinted systems and processes on a daily basis—will often have the best ideas about how to make things run even better.

Deliver WOW Service

"WOW!" That's what you want to hear your clients say *to* you and, more important, *about* you. At its heart, WOW service entails raising the bar to deliver each client a world-class experience—one that differentiates you and your firm in a way that clients find unforgettable and competitors find difficult to match. By creating processes that ensure a consistent, high-quality experience at every point of contact, you will evoke pure delight in your clients. And not *just* delight, but the motivation to provide you with more business. As **Exhibit 6.2** shows, the most satisfied, loyal clients give their advisors significantly more assets to manage and make many more qualified referrals than do less-satisfied clients.

When you WOW your clients to the extent that they not only give you all their assets to manage but also become your marketing apostles, you have arrived at an extremely effective way to build your

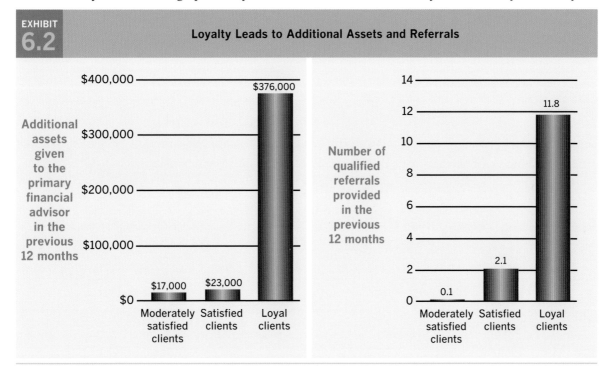

EXHIBIT 6.2

Loyalty Leads to Additional Assets and Referrals

N = 1,417 affluent individuals.
Source: Russ Alan Prince and David A. Geracioti, *Cultivating the Middle-Class Millionaire*, 2005.

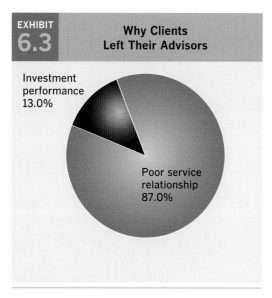

EXHIBIT 6.3

Why Clients Left Their Advisors

Investment performance 13.0%

Poor service relationship 87.0%

Source: Russ Alan Prince and Brett Van Bortel, *The Millionaire's Advisor™*, 2003.
Analysis: CEG Worldwide.

firm. And when you have delighted and loyal clients, their first thought every time they hear someone discussing financial services is to refer you.

And if you don't WOW your clients, you are quite likely to lose them. In Chapter 5 we saw that high-net-worth individuals typically have several advisors each. We also saw that when affluent clients move to a new advisor, it is not usually because they are unhappy with investment performance. As **Exhibit 6.3** vividly illustrates, a small minority of clients switch due to investment performance. This is a failure of fundamentals—their advisors failed to provide acceptable investment performance or adequate administrative and account service or both.

However, for the overwhelming majority of clients, there was a relationship failure—the clients were unhappy with the service their advisors provided. Those advisors may have met the clients' investment needs, but relationship failures drove them away. Ultimately, you must be the complete advisor your clients need—someone who can deliver satisfactory investment results and wealth management services and do so with a genuine and caring human touch.

What It Means to WOW

WOW is synonymous with *delight*, *dazzle* and *astound*. To build a world-class business, you must go much further than merely satisfying your clients. You can't just talk the customer satisfaction talk—you and everyone on your team who comes into contact with clients must live and breathe client satisfaction.

What would it mean for your firm to deliver WOW service? To answer this question, consider exactly what clients really need. **Exhibit 6.4** shows a three-step pyramid of affluent clients' hierarchy of needs.

Relationship satisfaction forms the base of the pyramid, and requires strong, ongoing personal interactions and connections between you and your affluent clients. Except in those rare cases when a client expresses a preference for minimal contact, it is essential to communicate more frequently with your clients—especially about something other than their investment accounts and performance. A recent survey we conducted showed that wealth managers, who, as you know from Chapter 4, earn much more than investment-oriented managers, contact each of their top 20 clients an average of 15.4 times per year, while investment-oriented managers only do so an average of 5.6 times.

Second on the pyramid, and built on top of relationship satisfaction, is **service satisfaction**. Affluent clients expect a high level of administrative and account service. If you frequently fail at these, your wealthy clients will most likely look for a new advisor. Given that problems will inevitably occur—however infrequently—you need constructive processes in place to quickly resolve these service failures.

Wealth management satisfaction sits at the top of the pyramid, supported by strong relationship and service satisfaction. The reason clients come to you in the first place is for assistance in solving their financial challenges and achieving their financial goals. An effective, comprehensive wealth management process is essential to address your clients' varied and often complex financial issues.

Relationship satisfaction forms the base of the pyramid for good reason. Clients who are unhappy with short-term investment performance are far more likely to

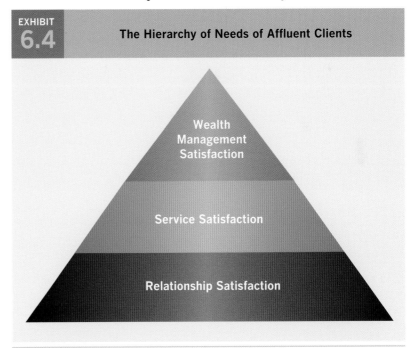

EXHIBIT 6.4 The Hierarchy of Needs of Affluent Clients

Wealth Management Satisfaction

Service Satisfaction

Relationship Satisfaction

Source: CEG Worldwide.

remain with you if they experience high relationship satisfaction. Likewise, a strong advisor-client relationship will help smooth out the inevitable bumps with respect to both service satisfaction and wealth management satisfaction. Therefore, we turn next to how to manage your client relationships to ensure relationship satisfaction.

The Seven Client Satisfaction Factors

Human relationships are complex, and no two client relationships are alike. Research has identified seven factors that are consistently aligned with a high level of client satisfaction. (See **Exhibit 6.5.**) To assess these factors, contrast the feelings of very satisfied clients with those of the very dissatisfied clients. Doing so will highlight the key elements of client satisfaction.

1. The Competence Factor

Managing the wealth of the affluent automatically assumes a reasonable level of financial and investment competence. For this reason, even clients who were very dissatisfied with their advisors were still likely to rate them high in the area of competence. For example, 80.6 percent of very dissatisfied clients gave their advisors credit for money management expertise—nearly the same as the 80.9 percent of very satisfied clients who did so. Very dissatisfied clients rated their advisors somewhat lower in the areas of confidentiality and knowledge about investments but still gave relatively high marks.

Since clients already assume competence, it's not a huge factor in determining client satisfaction. At the same time, this doesn't mean that you shouldn't justify your clients' view of your competence. Most of the items that you create through your credibility marketing efforts—including articles, white papers and books—will serve to reinforce your affluent clients' belief in your competence as a wealth manager.

2. The Hustle Factor

While competence is largely taken for granted, the same is not true of hustle—going the extra mile. This is seen most sharply in clients' views of their advisors' perfectionism. Fully 61.7 percent of very satisfied clients see their advisors as being perfectionists, compared with only 6.5 percent of very dissatisfied clients.

The key to high marks in hustle? Reliability. When you make a promise, keep it and keep it on time. Set a goal of providing perfect service, with plenty of attention to details.

3. The No-Surprises Factor

While clients dislike service failures, they dislike unpleasant surprises even more, making it your job to prevent them as much as possible. While more than half (55.3 percent) of very satisfied clients felt that their advisors wanted to hear their complaints and feedback, a mere 6.5 percent of very dissatisfied clients felt this way. Likewise, not a single very dissatisfied client believed that his or her advisor looked at failures as opportunities to provide better service by communicating about the problem and possible solutions, while 38.3 percent of very satisfied clients did.

To rate well with your clients in this area, you should actively solicit candid feedback, including negative perceptions, from your clients. Not only will this help you spot and head off major problems, it will clearly demonstrate

EXHIBIT 6.5	Seven Key Factors That Affect Client Satisfaction		
		Very Satisfied Clients	Very Dissatisfied Clients
The Competence Factor			
■ Keeping dealings confidential		82.6%	64.5%
■ Having money management expertise		80.9%	80.6%
■ Being knowledgeable in investments		72.3%	64.5%
The Hustle Factor			
■ Being extremely reliable		81.7%	54.8%
■ Being a perfectionist		61.7%	6.5%
The No-Surprises Factor			
■ Wanting to know complaints		55.3%	6.5%
■ Communicating about problems and solutions		38.3%	0.0%
The Warmth Factor			
■ Being responsive		74.9%	45.2%
■ Being warm		64.3%	25.8%
The First-to-Know Factor			
■ Providing timely information		77.9%	19.4%
■ Giving regular client briefings		75.3%	38.7%
The Listening Factor			
■ Being patient while explaining		82.6%	54.8%
■ Listening well		78.7%	48.4%
The Client-Centered Factor			
■ Understanding specific needs		75.7%	25.8%
■ Providing viable alternatives		75.3%	41.9%
■ Defining client needs		59.1%	12.9%

N = 879 affluent clients.

Source: Russ Alan Prince and Karen Maru File, *Cultivating the Affluent.*

your concern about service to your clients. In addition, whenever an external disaster occurs (such as the September 11, 2001, attacks), you'll do well to immediately get in touch—and stay in touch—with your clients.

4. The Warmth Factor

Responsiveness and sincere warmth are another important part of client satisfaction. Three-quarters (74.9 percent) of very satisfied clients saw their advisors as very responsive, compared with less than half (45.2 percent) of very dissatisfied clients. When asked if their advisors are warm, 64.3 percent of highly satisfied clients said yes, while only one-quarter of dissatisfied clients had this response.

It's important to understand that good manners and being polite are not enough—virtually all clients, satisfied and dissatisfied, believe that their advisors are generally courteous. Affluent clients are looking for more: true emotional warmth. Keep this in mind as you make your hiring decisions. If your staff (or you) needs help in this area, there are workshops that can help improve interpersonal skills, as will simply practicing these skills.

5. The First-to-Know Factor

Your clients want to be kept informed not just about their portfolios and financial progress, but also about important changes at your firm and with your staff. Don't let your clients hear about personnel changes when they are in need and call your office or from a competing advisor—this is exactly the type of negative surprise you want to avoid.

Very satisfied clients score their advisors well in this area, with 77.9 percent reporting that their advisors provided information in a timely manner, and 75.3 percent acknowledging their advisors' efforts to give regular briefings. As can be expected, very dissatisfied clients scored their advisors poorly here, with just 19.4 percent feeling that they received timely information from their advisors.

Given how important it is to affluent clients to be "first-to-know," it would be wise to incorporate tools into your client database that allow you to red-flag situations and issues that call for you to be in touch with clients.

6. The Listening Factor

As you well know by now, affluent clients want advisors who pay attention to them. Listening skills are therefore another important element in the client satisfaction equation. Of very satisfied clients, 82.6 percent thought that their advisors were willing to be patient and take as much time as needed to explain things, compared with 54.8 percent of dissatisfied clients. Likewise, a significantly greater number of satisfied clients believed their advisors spent enough time listening.

Too often advisors believe they must educate their clients, as opposed to listening to them as they speak of their needs, fears and wants. Your goal, as always, should be to learn more about your affluent clients through attentive listening.

7. The Client-Centered Factor

Affluent clients generally care little about your other clients. What they do care about is having you focus on them and their individual needs. Your ability to convey the sense to each client that you are striving to both understand his or her unique needs and then provide individualized solutions is absolutely critical.

Specifically, 75.7 percent of the satisfied clients felt that their advisors made a significant effort to understand their unique needs, as compared with only 25.8 percent of dissatisfied clients. Also revealing on this point: Three-quarters (75.3 percent) of the very satisfied thought they received well-thought-out solutions suited to their needs, contrasted with 41.9 percent of the dissatisfied.

The WOW Service Checklist

The following is a checklist of the factors that matter most to affluent clients and that lead to the highest levels of client satisfaction. The factors are grouped according to the three levels of the hierarchy of needs of affluent clients, starting at the bottom of the pyramid with relationship satisfaction, next moving up to service satisfaction and then to wealth management satisfaction. You can use the checklist both to evaluate your own current service level and as something to aim for in the future.

1. Relationship Satisfaction

- ❑ The advisor is emotionally warm and sympathetic and reassuring as needed.
- ❑ The advisor is honest and open at all times.
- ❑ The advisor is good at remembering personal details about clients.
- ❑ The advisor always keeps clients' interests at heart.
- ❑ The advisor always encourages clients to bring up any issue or question of importance.
- ❑ The advisor takes as much time as necessary to explain issues to clients yet never wastes clients' time.
- ❑ The advisor never shows impatience.
- ❑ The advisor spends an unusual amount of time listening closely to clients' needs, fears, wants and desires.
- ❑ The advisor does unexpected and thoughtful things for clients.
- ❑ The advisor and every firm member make each client feel extremely important.
- ❑ The advisor ascertains the type and frequency of contact each client wants and then provides exactly that contact.
- ❑ The advisor incorporates high-net-worth psychology into every contact.
- ❑ The advisor diplomatically handles communication mistakes made by clients.
- ❑ The advisor provides clients with ample information in writing as appropriate.
- ❑ The advisor provides each client with a detailed agenda for every meeting.
- ❑ The advisor introduces clients to qualified experts and other important individuals.
- ❑ The advisor provides regular updates about the firm's programs and operations.
- ❑ The advisor encourages clients to read the firm's promotional materials.
- ❑ The advisor actively encourages clients to suggest ways of improving operations and services.
- ❑ The advisor encourages clients to ask friends, family and associates about how they perceive the firm and its services.

2. Service Satisfaction

- ❑ The advisor always delivers within the promised time frame on the commitments he or she makes.
- ❑ Client accounts do not suffer from administrative errors.
- ❑ The advisor keeps all client information and dealings completely confidential.
- ❑ The advisor is always a perfectionist.
- ❑ The advisor involves each client in decision making to the extent the client prefers.
- ❑ Services are truly customized to fit the needs of each client.
- ❑ The advisor always provides timely information to every client.
- ❑ The advisor immediately gets in touch with clients when a major external event or disaster occurs.
- ❑ The advisor has a methodology in place to red-flag situations that require client contact.
- ❑ The firm's quality of service consistently exceeds client expectations.
- ❑ The advisor or staff member responds within the promised time frame to all client requests or telephone calls.
- ❑ The firm offers a dedicated toll-free phone line for clients.
- ❑ The firm offers a comprehensive user-friendly Web site that provides clients access to their portfolio information.
- ❑ The advisor gives quick and complete responses to all questions.
- ❑ The firm's or team's key professionals are highly accessible to clients.
- ❑ Staff members have appropriate access to client information to enable them to provide world-class service.
- ❑ The advisor frequently invites clients to provide feedback about the firm's or team's performance.
- ❑ The firm resolves all service failures in a timely fashion—when possible, on the same day they occur.
- ❑ The advisor views service failures as opportunities to provide great service by communicating about the problem and possible solutions.

❑ The advisor interviews all lost clients to determine and address their reasons for leaving.

❑ The firm occasionally uses an outside "mystery shopper" to assess levels of service and responsiveness.

❑ The firm periodically summarizes feedback on its own service performance and identifies areas of improvement.

3. Wealth Management Satisfaction

❑ The advisor makes an exceptional effort to understand each client's unique needs.

❑ The advisor works with all clients to define their needs in considerable detail.

❑ The advisor provides well-thought-out and viable alternatives suited to clients' specific needs, objectives and tolerance for risk.

❑ The advisor is knowledgeable about investments.

❑ Investment performance is consistent with clients' stated goals and objectives.

❑ Investment performance is good compared to indexes.

❑ Portfolio performance meets client expectations.

Assessing Client Satisfaction

To establish and then fine-tune your delivery of WOW service, you need help from your clients. It would be easy to assume that you already know how clients perceive your firm, but if you really want to know, you must proactively invite feedback.

To systematically collect this feedback, we recommend that you conduct a formal client survey every year. Such a survey gives your clients permission to point out where you could improve. It also sends a clear message that you care about them and their opinions, which will make them more willing to open up and help you explore how you can better serve them.

Start by using the WOW service checklist to identify the gaps between your current level of service and the WOW level. Then take the specific actions that will bring your service to a world-class level.

Once you've done this, ask your clients to complete a client satisfaction survey. (The design and details of such a survey are beyond the scope of this book but are available to participants in our coaching programs.) After you've gathered, organized and distilled the survey information, share the results with your team members. Get their reactions and input on improving systems in response to the survey results. While you won't always get positive responses from your surveys, every response can be used to your advantage in some way. Your whole business can become more responsive to your clients from the ground up.

Once you've created a list of action items in response to the survey results, communicate these to your clients. Let them know specifically how you will be doing things differently as a result of their input.

With a clear understanding in place of how to manage your practice as a business, we turn next to how to manage and best work with *other* businesses, from financial institutions and wholesalers to providers of technology and other noncore functions.

CHAPTER 7

Partner with Institutions and Other Professionals

Partner with Institutions and Other Professionals

As an entrepreneurial advisor, you can't create a great business all on your own—nor should you try. As we have stressed throughout this book, you and your clients will be far better off if you focus on your core competencies and outsource everything else. If you are like most successful advisors, this means outsourcing everything but client relationship management, expert relationship management and business development.

Such outsourcing makes sense for three very good reasons. First, industry research consistently shows that advisors who spend more time on these core competencies do better financially. Second, in today's complex world, providing your clients with a great experience and across-the-board WOW service requires a depth of expertise that is simply beyond any one individual or team. This means that your clients will directly benefit from intelligent outsourcing. And third, by being smart about which institutions, wholesalers, and other outside professionals and services you work with, you'll gain valuable practice management tips and uncover additional opportunities. In short, effective outsourcing enables you to focus on what really matters.

To become a great entrepreneur, you must learn to say "no" and to embrace the reality that you can't work with everyone who comes along. Instead, as we discussed in Chapter 3, you must only take on those clients who are right for you. With these ideal clients in place, you can focus on creating systems and processes that enable you to profitably and consistently deliver an experience that absolutely thrills and delights your clients.

Unfortunately, many advisors do not consciously choose their outsourcing partners. Instead, they end up working with particular institutions and other providers by accident and then become so busy with the day-to-day activities of their practices that they fail to take the time to consider what ideal partners would really look like.

As our industry has dramatically grown over the last decades, a wide variety of outside providers have made themselves readily available to assist financial advisors. Given the many potential providers who are competing for your business, if you're spending substantial time outside the scope of your core competencies, then you should make sure that you have a very compelling business reason for doing so. In this chapter, we will look at the two primary categories of outsourcing partners: financial institutions (and the wholesalers that work with them) and independent contractors.

Working with Financial Institutions and Their Wholesalers

All financial advisors—from wirehouse stockbrokers to independent broker-dealer representatives to registered investment advisors—work with financial institutions to one degree or another. At a minimum, you need custodial services from your brokerage firm or another custodian. To provide your clients with optimal solutions and WOW service, you need access to a variety of financial products and tools. As the idea of open architectures gains widespread acceptance, increasing numbers of advisors of all stripes are taking advantage of the benefits that come from working with multiple financial institutions.

Financial institutions are well aware that advisors have more choice than ever as to who to work with and that not all advisors are happy with what's been offered to date. As **Exhibit 7.1** shows,

EXHIBIT 7.1

Investment Companies Must Do More

Advisors who believe that investment companies will have to do more than ever before to win advisor loyalty

- Registered investment advisors: 89.4%
- Independent broker-dealer representatives: 79.0%
- Brokers with wirehouses: 78.5%

N = 2,094 advisors.
Source: CEG Worldwide, 2007.

the great majority of advisors who were surveyed believe that investment companies will need to do more in the future to win advisor loyalty.

As financial products become ever more commoditized, financial institutions recognize that they must rely on more than the quality of their products to differentiate themselves in the minds of advisors. To do so, they offer support and services designed to help advisors grow their businesses and serve their clients better and more profitably. Commonly called "value-based marketing," this support, usually offered through the financial institution's wholesalers, is provided in three main areas:

1. **Sales and marketing:** helping advisors move upmarket by attracting affluent clients
2. **Practice management support:** disseminating the best practices of advisors to help them build more profitable businesses
3. **Technical support:** assistance with technical issues concerning the financial institution's products and services

Regardless of which financial institutions you are working with now—or are considering working with in the future—be thoughtful and choose your partners for the right reasons. Being able to accurately evaluate the offerings of institutions so that you can select the right ones will make a critical difference to the success of your business.

Identifying the Right Financial Institutions

To determine whether your current institutional partners are optimal for your practice, start with some self-analysis. We recommend using a consultative process similar to the one that we recommend you use with your clients to assist them in achieving their financial goals. Examine your practice and evaluate any existing or potential partners with the following four-step process.

Step 1. Be Introspective

Examine the quantitative part of your business. Identify your results over the last 12 months. Write down your net income, assets under management, assets that you influence and gross revenue. Also identify the number of client relationships, the number of referrals you've obtained and the number of group presentations you've conducted during the last year.

Identify your current value proposition to your clients. What feedback do you receive from prospects and clients regarding your service offerings? Which additional elements will you need to significantly increase your business?

What would a new institutional partner bring to your business that your current partners are not offering? How would a new partner address the feedback you've identified and provide the additional elements you need to meet the needs of your current and future clients?

Step 2. Develop a Clear Vision of Your Future

Is what you're doing today really what matters to you in the long run? Many of us get caught up in our ongoing activities and forget to focus on what's really important in our business and personal lives. What matters most gets buried under layers of pressing problems, immediate concerns and to-do lists. If you are serious about building a hugely successful business, you cannot afford to get lost in the mundane of the day-to-day.

Revisit the vision for your future that we recommended you develop. Do your current institutional partners fit into this picture? Do they actively support your vision? Or are they stumbling blocks to achieving it?

Step 3. Identify Goals Important to Realizing Your Vision

Make a list of the personal and business goals that are important to your vision and that you will commit to achieving over the next year. To be most effective, write down your commitments. Now ask yourself: Would changing any of my institutional partners increase the probability of achieving my goals?

Step 4. Evaluate Potential Partners

If your assessment reveals that your current partners are not optimal for building a world-class business, your next task is to identify partners who *can* fill that role for you. Accurately evaluating the offerings of financial institutions so that you can select the right ones will have a tremendous positive impact on your business. At the core of your decisions are two key questions:

1. Is the financial institution equipped to help me properly serve my market? You need to work with institutions that can support your move to a significantly higher level of success by enabling you to better serve your affluent clients.

2. If not, are the deficiencies severe enough to warrant moving to a new one? The time and money required to move to a new financial institution can be significant (this is particularly true of a switch to a new broker-dealer or clearing firm), so do not undertake a move without being sure that you can justify the costs.

These are not easy questions. To help you answer them, methodically assess the value proposition of your current financial institutions or of any institutions that you are considering partnering with. Your goal is to identify the institutions that will provide you and your clients the most net value, or the value gained minus the costs.

First assess the total value to you that an institution will provide, including these elements:

- Product value
- Service value
- Personnel value
- Image value

Then add up the total cost to you of working with that institution. Consider these costs:

- Monetary cost
- Time cost
- Energy cost
- Psychic cost

Finally, subtract the total costs from the total value that you receive, and you'll be in a much better position to make a final determination as to the institution in question. At that point, the choice is yours as to which institutions are right to serve as partners for you and your clients. Remember we are all judged by the company we keep.

Identifying the Right Wholesalers

Once you've chosen the best institutional partners to support your success, you can expect the wholesalers (often called "business development managers" or "business consultants") who represent these institutions to call on you. More often than not, you won't have a choice about the specific wholesalers you'll work with. Instead your choice will be whether you work with an assigned wholesaler or directly with the institution's internal wholesaler group.

As the go-between who connects companies offering financial products and services and the advisors who ultimately recommend those products and services to clients, wholesalers are an inevitable part of life in our business. Many financial advisors regard wholesalers as either a nuisance or a source of ongoing freebies. The overall advisor experience with wholesalers has been, at best, mixed. CEG Worldwide research conducted in 2007 found that working with a top-flight wholesaler was a concern for just half of 2,094 studied advisors. Of those working with mutual fund wholesalers, just 28.0 percent rated these wholesalers as "very good" or "excellent."

Despite this mixed experience, wholesalers can be invaluable resources and potent business-building partners—provided that you screen for the best ones and then work with them to maximum advantage. If you are proactive about identifying and working with the "A" players who have the ability to provide you with substantial value, you'll have serious business development partners who can help you build a truly great practice.

How, then, can you differentiate between wholesalers? To begin with, consider the differences between the three prominent wholesaler strategies:

1. **The educational strategy** includes value-based marketing programs, chiefly characterized by technical, prospecting, sales, practice management and other programs that are delivered through the wholesaler system.
2. **The field support strategy** focuses on your sales and marketing processes. Wholesalers can work with one of your clients directly or, at the other end of the continuum, develop comprehensive, targeted marketing materials for you to use with your clients.
3. **The consultative strategy** takes a much more intensive approach. Often wholesalers become

business and practice management consultants to you, providing you with counsel on key aspects of your business by using the full resources of their financial institutions.

While these three value-based marketing strategies are not mutually exclusive, many financial institutions have decided to primarily focus on just one. Once you are clear about which type of strategy will deliver the most value to you and your clients, you can focus on developing relationships with the wholesalers who mainly follow that strategy.

As a general rule, we recommend that you focus on working with wholesalers who embrace the consultative approach. You want ongoing relationships with a small number of wholesalers who serve as outside business partners by providing you with valuable insight into how other successful advisors are growing their businesses. As "how-to-grow-your-business coaches" who serve as conduits of best practices and leverage their financial institutions' resources, these wholesalers can help you substantially grow your business and better serve your clients.

However, the educational and field support strategies can yield substantial value in certain circumstances. For example, if you have a client with a large concentrated stock position and neither you nor anyone on your team is well-versed in all the options available to deal effectively, then a good wholesaler may be able to quickly provide you with access to an in-house expert. Ultimately, as the wholesaler market matures, we believe that all three strategies will more and more frequently be used together to develop strong, multifaceted support programs.

The bottom line: Regardless of which strategy they follow, there are extremely qualified wholesalers out there who can be of tremendous assistance to you—but you need to be intentional about identifying them and working with them effectively. To recognize the best wholesalers, once again you should begin with the end in mind and remember to place a great premium on your time—it's the one thing that you can never get back. Since your core competencies do not include responding to copious wholesaler phone calls or selecting the best possible wholesalers to work with, your first step is to train an assistant or someone in your office to undertake these activities.

When wholesalers call you—and they will—the screener should say something like this: "Mr. Smith works with a limited number of top wholesalers, so it's very important to him that wholesalers deliver a significant value in terms of helping him grow his business. I'd like to ask you a few questions to make sure your time with him would be well-spent." Such questions would include the following:

- "How do you typically work with financial advisors?"
- "Have you ever been a financial advisor? How does your previous experience help you meet the challenges that Mr. Smith faces?"
- "What kind of support do you typically provide to advisors?"
- "Can you give me some examples of best practices that you have shared with advisors who are working with [the advisor's specific target market]?"
- "Can you share some of the best sales ideas of the top advisors you work with that might be applicable to Mr. Smith's practice?"
- "Mr. Smith typically works on a consultative basis; rather than focusing on product sales, he works with each client through a systematic consulting process. How can you help him improve his consulting process while using your financial products?"
- "To what extent can you provide assistance in leading-edge, highly technical areas of wealth management to help Mr. Smith serve his clients better?"
- "Do you or does someone in your company provide additional practice management support that will help Mr. Smith run his business more efficiently and profitably?"
- "To what extent can you be Mr. Smith's personal coach to help him achieve all that he is capable of achieving?"

If it becomes clear that the wholesaler mainly follows the educational strategy or field support strategy as opposed to the consultative strategy, you can also have the screener ask questions more specifically attuned to these strategies, such as these:

- "Please describe the level of product knowledge you have, not only of your company's products but also of your competitors' products."
- "To what extent can you provide me with competitive information on products similar to yours?"
- "To the extent that Mr. Smith offers seminars for prospects and clients, what tools do you

offer—such as well-designed group presentations—that have been particularly effective in working with affluent clients?"

■ "Are you available for one-on-one sales presentations to select prospects or clients when appropriate?"

The screener can end the call by saying, "Thanks for answering these questions. I'll check with Mr. Smith, consult the calendar and then get back to you." The screener should then prepare a short summary of the call. In some cases, the screener might be very clear that this is not a wholesaler you want to work with, but in most cases you'll need to make the final decision. Sometimes, it will be obvious that the wholesaler has nothing to offer beyond his or her own firm's product information. In most of these cases you'll want to call the wholesaler back and politely decline the meeting, unless the product information being offered is directly on point for your target niche or otherwise fills a critical knowledge gap (such as in our concentrated stock position example above).

Having identified the wholesalers you want to meet with in person, once again it pays to prepare. Before your meeting, create a written agenda and send it in advance by email. Given the screening process, the wholesaler will already be aware that your expectations surpass those of most advisors. Still, by putting forward specific topics of discussion and deliverables, you are more likely to begin to build the consultative coaching relationship you want.

Of course, you must respect the wholesaler's purpose as well and allow him or her to tell you about the company, products and recent enhancements in the context of assisting you in building your wealth management business. Remember that your goal is to forge a business partnership with a select number of top wholesalers who can truly make a difference in your success.

Your screening process and agenda may not be the norm, but it probably won't be a first for the wholesaler. Moreover, good wholesalers will rise to the occasion when they know that they've got a top advisor to potentially work with—someone who knows the difference between a free lunch (or a dozen golf balls) and a real relationship. At the end of the day, the best wholesalers want to work with the most successful advisors. Only the best wholesalers will be able to meet your expectations, and those are the ones you want to work with. Most successful advisors have five or fewer wholesalers whom they regularly see.

Getting the Most from Your Wholesaler Relationships

Even working with the best wholesalers, it's still up to you to get the most value possible from these relationships. The following three actions will help you to optimize each of your wholesaler relationships.

Use Field Support Carefully

Just because a wholesaler offers a service does not always mean that you should use it. For example, while many wholesalers are happy to make seminar presentations for you (or together with you), you should generally forgo this route. Your goal is to build relationships with presentation attendees, making it counterproductive for someone beyond your expert team or strategic alliances to do the talking. Of course, if the wholesaler is a true master at giving presentations, it may make sense to share the stage with him or her a few times in order to enhance your skill set through real-time tutoring and feedback.

As another example, wholesalers may also offer to close cases on your behalf. While this might be tempting, it detracts from your positioning as the advisor who solves the challenges of clients in your niche market. Industry research shows that this particular lesson is clear to elite advisors. One CEG Worldwide study found that nearly half (46.2 percent) of lower-income advisors want wholesalers in the field who can close cases for them, while only 7.1 percent of higher-income advisors want this type of support.

Provide Feedback

Since wholesalers are one of the most costly advisor support tools available, financial institutions want them to be used effectively. It's up to you to tap into these resources and let your product sponsors know when you get great service and when you do not. Smart financial institutions will be responsive to your feedback.

Focus First on a Small Project

You should focus on one key project first so that all involved parties can win—your practice will grow as you serve your clients well, and the wholesaler will share in your success as you increase your assets under management. Remember that wholesalers act in their own enlightened self-interest. Like top advisors, top wholesalers can only work with a limited number of clients. The best ones choose their advisors carefully based on the level of success they expect those advisors to have.

Outsourcing or Delegating Everything Else

Running your business requires many types of skills apart from pure relationship building and business development. You are often pulled back and forth between back-office problems and client opportunities, with a significant impact on your profitability. You can avoid nearly all these distractions, however, by applying the rule of the four D's to every task, in this order:

1. **Drop it.** If there is no compelling business reason to spend time on a task—either your time or your staff's time—then drop it. When it comes to non-revenue activities, you can nearly always drop them.

2. **Defer it.** If you are unsure whether a task will result in a positive benefit for your clients or your practice, defer it. Schedule a time to re-evaluate it, and make a decision at that time to drop it, delegate it or do it.

3. **Delegate it.** When a task lies clearly outside of your core competencies, delegate it, either to a staff person or to an outsourcing partner.

4. **Do it.** If a task is part of one of your core competencies and if none of the previous three D's are appropriate, then—and only then—do it.

If you run your business efficiently, you will find that you are able to delegate every function outside of your core competencies. To delegate at this high level, you will almost certainly need to outsource at least some of your business functions.

The Importance of Outsourcing

Outsourcing is critical because it allows you to do more of what really matters: building relationships with your existing clients, managing your expert relationships and starting relationships with potential clients. The underlying rationale is as simple as it is compelling: Spending more time with these people leads to more income.

Industry research confirms the very real impact that spending time with clients has on your income. As **Exhibit 7.2** shows, fewer than one in ten advisors spend more than 60 percent of their time in front of clients. Most advisors spend between 30 percent and 60 percent of their time in front of clients, while a substantial minority (28.1 percent) spend less than 30 percent of their time with clients.

As you can see in **Exhibit 7.3**, those few advisors who do spend more than 60 percent of their time in client-facing activities enjoy annual incomes that are more than *three times* those of advisors spending 30 percent to 60 percent of their time with clients and nearly *six times* those of advisors who spend less than 30 percent of their time in front of clients. Time truly is money.

Preferred Outsourcing Options

As we saw in Chapter 6, using technology wisely frees you from myriad administrative tasks. But technology is only one part of the solution. Finding and managing qualified independent contractors to whom you can outsource a variety of tasks is the other.

There are two preferred options. The first is to outsource everything you can to either your broker-dealer or to your turnkey asset management program (TAMP). This is the best outsourcing alternative.

However, if your financial institution partner cannot meet these needs, you can turn to the second option, which is to outsource specific noncore functions to independent providers on an as-needed basis. This is your classic "make or buy" (or in this case, "rent") decision.

EXHIBIT 7.2	Work Time Spent in Client-Facing Activities	
Percentage		**All Financial Advisors**
More than 60%		9.1%
30–60%		62.8%
Less than 30%		28.1%

N = 463 advisors.
Source: *Advisor 2000*. Analysis: CEG Worldwide.

EXHIBIT 7.3	More Time with Clients Means Greater Average Net Income	
Percentage		**All Financial Advisors**
More than 60%		$160,500
30–60%		$50,300
Less than 30%		$27,800

N = 463 advisors.
Source: *Advisor 2000*. Analysis: CEG Worldwide.

Determining What You Will Outsource

The first step in successful outsourcing is to identify what you can call on others to do. Your job is to determine which tasks you will do yourself, which you will rely on an institutional partner to do and which you will need independent contractors to do.

As we saw in our discussion on blueprinting systems and processes, you should describe and document every function in your business. Revisit your blueprints to help identify the specific tasks that would be more effectively or profitably completed by an outsourcing partner than by an in-house staffer.

We have found that the most successful advisors frequently outsource the following seven systems:

1. Advanced planning
2. Business development
3. Back office
4. Compliance
5. Technology
6. Public relations
7. Team building

At an enterprise level, we find that additional systems may also be candidates for outsourcing. These include the hiring system, the planning system, the evaluation and compensation systems, the rewards and recognition system, and the measurement system, among others.

Effective Outsourcing

More and more advisors are turning to independent contractors—freelancers—to fill many of their non-client relationship tasks and, as a result, are enjoying higher profit margins and better quality control. They are finding that such independent contractors are often much more focused and committed to successfully completing projects than are employees.

Even though independent contractors do offer many advantages, they also present a new set of challenges when it comes to finding, hiring and managing them. We recommend undertaking the following three stages and the specific actions within each stage to make your outsourcing as successful as possible.

Stage 1: Planning

1. **Define your needs.** Decide exactly what you will outsource. Pull together your current costs of doing each function in-house. Be clear on the results you hope to achieve by outsourcing (such as lower costs, improved performance, enhanced service or overall responsiveness). If it's a large outsourcing project, design a request for proposal (RFP) that includes performance metrics, evaluation criteria, a scoring process and a financial model to evaluate price or cost.
2. **Define the needed skills.** Determine the specific skills that you'll need in an independent contractor before you start searching for one. Most individuals specialize, so don't expect to find a broad range of diverse skills in any one person (and if you do, expect to pay very well for it).
3. **Anticipate issues.** Take a moment to think through the effect on your business of outsourcing this particular function. If necessary, act to head off any potential issues or problems.

Stage 2: Selection

4. **Obtain referrals.** Because more and more advisors are moving toward virtual offices, they can be your best source of referrals for high-quality independent contractors with experience in the financial services industry.
5. **Interview candidates.** Identify the most qualified candidates and interview them. Again, if it's a large project, evaluate the candidates' proposals in response to your RFP.
6. **Check references.** When you've identified a good candidate, always ask for references. Check each of those references, and make sure to ask if they know whom else that independent contractor is working with—and place a call to those firms as well. Often you will get a very different and much more insightful perspective because these additional references will not have been preselected by the independent contractor.
7. **Create a good fit with existing staff.** Independent contractors should complement your exist-

ing team by bringing in new expertise and talent. They should not displace or alienate your team by being brought in for interesting projects that your current staff is perfectly capable of doing a good job with. Simply duplicating existing skills will only erode the morale of your permanent team and gain you little. Where appropriate, involve your staff in independent contractor hiring decisions.

8. **Select your new provider.** When choosing among two or three finalists, be sure to weigh the relationship factor in your final selection. Expertise is key, but so are credibility and chemistry.

Stage 3: Implementation

9. **Negotiate the written contract.** Once you've chosen the leading candidate, negotiate the details of your contract. Create a clear agreement that defines the project, deliverables, deadlines and benchmarks. It should spell out the billing and payment process and deal with any intellectual property issues and noncompete provisions. An employment attorney can draft a boilerplate agreement that you can use over and over.

10. **Start slowly.** As you begin working with an independent contractor, start with bite-size pieces. Assign a meaningful project (but not one that is mission-critical) for which you might pay in the low four figures, to assess the contractor's performance. If you are forced to outsource a mission-critical project to an unfamiliar contractor, you can evaluate the contractor on the fly much as you would a potential employee. Hire the contractor as a consultant to put together a plan for how he or she would complete the project in the assigned time frame. Have the person talk to clients and internal staff as appropriate and then present his or her solution to you.

11. **Manage and monitor.** Be clear about expectations, but don't micromanage. Let freelancers be freelancers, and allow them to freely use their own expertise and creativity to achieve high-quality results. Give them access to internal staff and resources as needed. Set up a clear channel of communication, preferably with a single point person in your firm, so that you can be apprised of project progress and so that your independent contractors can keep current with any changes in the firm that affect projects. Give them every opportunity to succeed.

12. **Pay promptly.** We all appreciate being paid promptly. If independent contractors are diligent about completing their projects in a timely manner, they will be justifiably irked if you then take too much time to process their invoices. And you'll quickly get a reputation as a slow payer among the network of freelancers, making it more difficult for you to bring on good talent.

A Checklist for Conscious Partnering

Whether you are considering working with a financial institution, wholesaler or independent contractor, evaluate and choose each one deliberately and systematically. Ask yourself these questions:

- ❏ Am I effectively outsourcing everything that I can—and should—so that I can focus on my core competencies?
- ❏ Given my chosen clientele and market niche, do I have the right number and quality of external relationships in place?
- ❏ Am I deep-down satisfied with the financial institutions that I rely upon for critical services such as custody of clients' funds and the products and services that I offer?
- ❏ Have I created a system for screening the wholesalers I want to work with? Do I use it effectively?
- ❏ Am I making the most effective and most efficient use of each of my external relationships, whether with a financial institution, a wholesaler, or a third-party service or product provider?
- ❏ Do I have a good system in place for identifying, hiring, managing and paying independent contractors?
- ❏ Have I made it a priority to regularly (at least annually) review all my external relationships?

The last item on this checklist points to the need to make good, proactive, business-building choices on an ongoing basis. Even if you've been diligent, whatever you know (or *think* you know) right now is unlikely to include everything that you will actually need to know in six months or a year. To succeed as an entrepreneurial advisor to the affluent, you need to commit to lifelong (or at least career-long) learning, which we turn to in the next chapter.

CHAPTER 8

Commit to Lifelong Learning

Commit to Lifelong Learning

To become an elite advisor in our rapidly evolving industry, you must commit to lifelong learning. It's as simple as that. Not only will your clients expect you to stay abreast of important developments, but today's regulatory environment demands that you stay up to date. And you obviously want to give yourself every possible advantage as you grow your business. Ongoing learning will give you this edge.

We suggest that you focus on two distinct areas of learning:

- **Practice management issues.** What are the best practices of top advisors? How can you implement these practices in your own business? What's new and valuable that you shouldn't miss? How can you more effectively move upmarket? What critical new research must you know about?

- **Strategic wealth management knowledge.** With regard to everything from asset allocation and portfolio construction to tax management strategies and legal developments, it's important to keep current on the state of the art in wealth management. You are looking here not so much for in-depth knowledge of advanced planning areas as a high-level overview of sophisticated concepts in order to flag your clients' issues and leverage the right experts to provide optimal solutions.

We recommend two very different types of activities to address these two areas. The first is to work with a mentor, coach or consultant. The second is to create a formal learning program for yourself and your staff. We'll specifically describe how to go about these activities, but keep in mind these general guidelines:

- **Conduct a self-review:** Start with a frank assessment of where you and your staff are now and where there are gaps in your knowledge and skills. Which educational activities would fill in these gaps so you can deliver even better service and solutions to your clients?

- **Be steady and consistent:** Lifelong learning is not a sprint but a never-ending journey toward an ever-growing summit of knowledge. Take your time, engage in the learning process in the most effective ways you can (this is not an area where you can afford to cut costs) and remember to enjoy yourself along the way.

■ **Pay attention to the knowing-doing gap:** As we discussed in Chapter 2, the knowing-doing gap presents a pervasive challenge for all of us. Knowledge by itself won't do you any good; you have to know how to use it well. Unfortunately, many corporate-style training programs dispense a great deal of intellectual knowledge but offer little in the way of actual application. When you go back to the office and try to employ what you've learned, you'll often find that things are very different than in the training course and that implementing effective and lasting change takes more than just knowing how to do something.

Working with a Mentor, Coach or Consultant

A good mentor, coach or consultant will help you create a vision of what you want your life and practice to be and then help you achieve it. This individual will enable you to start thinking of your time horizon as many years, not just a few months. Just as elite athletes have coaches who help ensure their best performances, a coach, mentor or consultant can be a true partner who holds you accountable for living up to your full potential.

Even more, a good coach, mentor or consultant can help you fill in the gaps in your competencies; keep up with developments in your area of expertise; and apply your new knowledge, in real time, in your specific business environment, thus helping you to surmount the knowing-doing gap. An effective mentor, coach or consultant—someone who can provide both knowledge and a formal "learning and doing" structure to support what you want to achieve—can therefore play a vital role in your efforts to build a world-class wealth management business.

Six Steps to Leveraging Mentors, Coaches and Consultants

To optimize your relationship with a coach, mentor or consultant, we highly recommend the following six steps:

Step 1. Perform a Self-Assessment

Before anything else, sit down and have a serious conversation with yourself. Ask yourself: What is it that you *really* want? Imagine yourself in the future: What do you want your life to look like in one year? Five years? Twenty years? Don't limit yourself to what you want to achieve in business, but look at the entire picture, including your family life, your leisure time and your health. Remember we are in business to build the quality of life we want. Compare where you are now to where you want to go. What do you need to get there? What are your major concerns?

Make this a serious self-assessment and be as objective as you possibly can. It will help to look at yourself as your spouse or a close friend might see you. The willingness to perform this kind of candid self-assessment is a clear indication that you have the commitment that a good coach or mentor will require.

Step 2. Define Your Areas of Focus

Using your self-assessment, and looking back at Chapter 6's work on creating a compelling vision and business plan, define the specific areas where you want to change or improve over the next 12 months. For example, you might want to work with affluent clients who have at least $2 million in investable assets each. In addition, you may want to implement systems that will elevate your client service in order to increase your assets under management and net profit by a certain percentage. You might also include areas from your personal life that you identified in your self-assessment.

Step 3. Choose Between a Mentor, a Coach or a Consultant

Once you have a clear idea of what you'd like to achieve, you'll be in a position to ask: Who might help me with these particular issues? Who can offer me optimal assistance? Mentors, coaches and consultants each bring unique qualities to the table.

Mentors are ideal to work with because the right one will have already attained the level of success that you want to achieve and will help you realize the same or even greater success. The best mentor will already be a leading advisor, will have already traveled the road you are now traveling, and will have great experiences and in-depth knowledge that he or she is willing to share with you.

Unfortunately, there are just not that many mentors available in our industry. Many financial institutions and some trade associations try to foster mentoring, but it is usually designed for advisors just getting started or for those in the midmarket. At the high end of the market, finding a mentor really comes down to personal relationships. If you know and like someone who has already achieved substantial success, then you should definitely consider asking him or her to be your mentor. Mentors are typically not compensated at all or at most receive nominal compensation. Still, you'll want to establish some type of formal relationship where you get together in person or speak on the phone on a regular basis.

However, unless you are very lucky or very gifted in developing relationships (or both), you are unlikely to have access to a true mentor other than for short periods during your career. Instead, you'll probably need to engage either a coach or a consultant.

Coaches may or may not have expertise in the financial world. Instead, they are experts in helping you identify what you want, creating a plan to achieve your goals, and enabling you to keep your energy and focus sustained over time to arrive at your destination. As with a mentor, a coach will work with you on a long-term basis. Because coaches typically work over the phone, you'll have no geographic restrictions. In our experience, if you work with a competent coach, especially one with expertise in financial services, you can expect that in the first 12 months you'll see at least a 25 percent growth in both your net income and assets under management.

Consultants are typically brought in for the short term to solve a specific challenge. These challenges usually revolve around strategy, marketing and other big-picture items that you need to address before you can move forward. These might include your firm's structure or strategic positioning, a merger or acquisition, or your technology system. Consultants have expertise in areas that you do not and can thus add greatly to your skill set, particularly in areas that are beyond your core competencies. Because consultants work with you over a defined period on one or more

Coaching Programs Offered by CEG Worldwide

As we describe at the end of this book, CEG Worldwide offers coaching programs for advisors who want to break through to a substantially higher level of success by serving high-net-worth clients. Each program provides in-depth learning and intensive coaching on the key strategies and tactics needed for success. Our expectation is that by the time advisors complete these programs, they will see their assets under management grow by at least 30 percent, and many advisors will enjoy growth well in excess of 50 percent.

specific challenges, the nature of your relationship with a consultant will be fundamentally different than with a mentor or coach.

Step 4. Choose the Right Individual

Once you've decided whether a mentor, coach or consultant is most appropriate for your situation, take these four actions to locate and evaluate candidates:

1. **Identify candidates.** Whom do you most admire in the field where you wish to excel? Who is enjoying the most success? Many successful advisors have coaches, mentors or consultants and can offer you referrals.

2. **Get in touch.** Ask the candidate how he or she was able to succeed. You want to find out not just what the individual knows, but also whether he or she is someone you can learn from. He or she should be able to engage you in a way that connects with you and touches on your ambitions. Someone may be a top expert in the field, but if you don't feel a personal connection, that person is not right for you.

3. **Interview.** You'll want to interview each candidate to find out whether his or her skill set meets your needs and your personalities mesh. Ask about his or her background and specifically about having worked with someone in your situation with goals similar to your own. Because it's easier to understand an approach by actually experiencing it—rather than just describing it—many coaches, mentors and consultants will offer you a free practice coaching session.

4. **Ask.** If you feel that a particular person might be a good coach or mentor, ask whether he or she would be willing to work with you in your area. If the individual is not a good match, ask for a referral to someone who might be.

If you are searching for a **coach** or **mentor**, keep these things in mind as you talk to candidates:

■ **The relationship is key.** You, not the coach or mentor, should always be the center of attention. You should feel powerful in this context and feel recharged after each session. This will help you sustain your momentum between meetings.

■ **You should feel safe and courageous with your coach or mentor.** Be open to exploring new ideas and opportunities that you would normally avoid. You must be willing to take risks with this person. Only when you take risks will new opportunities open for you.

- **The relationship must be confidential.** You should never have to worry about sharing information with your coach or mentor.

- **There must be trust on both sides.** You must believe that the coach or mentor is truly on your side and believes that you will do what you say you will do.

- **There must be honesty.** The coaching or mentoring relationship must be one in which you are able to tell the whole truth about yourself without concern about looking good or being judged. You should also expect that your coach or mentor will speak the unvarnished truth about you as he or she sees it. The relationship is not about being nice. It's about being direct and effective.

> ### Sources for Coaches, Mentors and Consultants
>
> The **International Coach Federation (ICF)** (www.coachfederation.org) is a worldwide professional association of thousands of business and personal coaches. It offers a free referral service, and its Web site lists many coaches, including those who specialize in financial services and business development.
>
> The **Professional Coaches and Mentors Association (PCMA)** (www.pcmaonline.com) is an association of business and organizational coaches and mentors. Many of its members are senior people who have a high degree of professionalism and are typically of a higher grade than ICF members.

- **The coach or mentor should be able to make bold requests yet not be attached to outcomes.** The outcomes are yours. The coach or mentor is there to help you achieve the ones you choose.

On the other hand, if you've decided to work with a **consultant**, look for someone who has demonstrated success in working with firms like yours. Note that just like top advisors, the best consultants get their business through relationship marketing, especially referrals from your peers, financial institutions and strategic allies. Finally, don't work with a consultant who does not have industry-specific experience—you'll end up paying that person to learn the business on your time.

Step 5. Make an Agreement and Action Plan

Your goal is to close the gap between what you have and what you want. Most coaches, mentors and consultants will want to work within the framework of a very clear agreement about the results you want to achieve within a specified time frame. This agreement will precisely define your ambitions—what you are truly passionate about and are willing—even eager—to work hard to achieve.

We often get caught up in things that we think we ought to be doing, usually as defined by someone else. Simply wanting something because it sounds like something we *should* want is not enough. A skilled individual will help you get in touch with your real ambitions and will do so in a nonjudgmental way.

You should also create a detailed action plan that will identify the steps you will take and the barriers you might encounter. Your coach, mentor or consultant will gauge how much confidence you have in actually accomplishing each step and will help you craft a realistic plan.

Step 6. Work Your Plan

Many coaches, mentors and consultants will want you to make a minimum commitment—typically six months to a year—in which some real work can get done. During this assessment period, examine your progress. Are you making the improvements you want? Do you have the ambition to move forward or are you feeling pushed along? Are you enthusiastic about continuing the process or do you feel resistance? Assuming that the process is working for you, move ahead.

When you bump into barriers on the path, a coach, mentor or consultant will help you see the difference between obstacles that are actually outside of you and those that are within you. This will help get you around barriers that otherwise might have stopped your progress. If you don't meet your goals, he or she will help you learn from this and to determine what you can do differently.

A good coach, mentor or consultant will also help reveal things to you about yourself that you may never have noticed. By uncovering these blind spots, you'll be able to make choices and see opportunities that you previously might have missed. Perhaps most valuable of all, this person can help you start to understand that your ambitions are larger—and more attainable—than you ever thought.

Establish a Formal Learning Program

In addition to working with a coach, mentor or consultant, we urge you to establish a formal learning program for both yourself and your staff. Such a program will keep you and your staff up to date on changing markets and client needs as well as on evolving products and services.

Many types of learning programs are readily available, including these:

- **Programs provided by financial institutions.** As we discussed in Chapter 7, aim to take advantage of the financial institutions that offer you and your staff substantial support and training.

- **Designations offered by industry associations.** Depending on your goals, it may be appropriate for you and/or senior members of your staff to pursue some of the worthwhile designations, including, but not limited to, Certified Financial Planner (CFP), Chartered Financial Analyst (CFA) and Certified Investment Management Analyst (CIMA).

- **Learning programs presented by industry organizations.** Many industry professional associations, including the Financial Planning Association, the National Association of Fee-Only Planners and the Investment Management Consultants Association, convene annual national and regional conferences, as well as offer e-learning programs, covering specific areas or expertise.

Six Steps to an Effective Learning Program

Your learning program should be well-planned and formalized. A hit-and-miss approach will yield hit-and-miss results—something you can't afford. Since your staff is integral to your efforts, include them in your program. And importantly, with respect to spending time and money on ongoing learning, don't be "penny-wise and pound-foolish." Wise investments in training and learning are essential to your long-term success in building a world-class business.

We suggest the following six steps to establish an effective learning program:

Step 1. Identify Areas for Development and Areas of Strength

Given the costs of training—in both time and money—you want to focus on precisely those issues that will provide the greatest results. Consider any weak links and areas that could benefit from special attention, especially gaps in skills relevant to delivering a superlative client experience. Where do people need help in addressing challenges? Also, who shines at particular tasks? Would it be worthwhile to enhance these strengths even farther?

Step 2. Identify Specific Areas of Focus

Examine each area to determine the specific skills, knowledge or experience that you or your staff must acquire in order to address those areas. For example, as your firm's or team's rainmaker, you may need to take a public speaking class or work with a consultant who specializes in highly effective presentations. Or if you have a staff member struggling with a particular technology tool, a one-day class could solve the problem.

Step 3. Identify Specific Learning Events

Once you've identified the specific areas where both you and individual staff members will focus, determine the particular events, classes or groups that you or your staff members will attend or take part in. Because any program will take valuable time away from your business, be sure to establish in advance whether it has a high likelihood of delivering the learning experience you need. Spend a few minutes on the phone with program providers to find out exactly what they offer. Ask for references of other advisors (or their staff members) who have taken part in the same program. If the expertise or tools aren't exactly what you need—if they are unlikely to add real value—then politely decline.

Step 4. Map Out the Learning Program

Chart out your learning activities for the next 12 months. Post it in your office so that everyone is clear on which issues are being addressed, how and when. Enter the activities on your electronic intra-office calendar if you have one.

Step 5. Take Part in All Learning Activities

Make your attendance and that of your staff a top priority at every scheduled learning opportunity. Set an example by meticulously monitoring your own attendance and participation, and make sure your staff knows that you expect their best efforts as well.

Step 6. Apply What You Have Learned

Systematically integrate new knowledge into the services you offer to your clients. Having spent the time and money needed to acquire this knowledge, make sure that you leverage it to add maximum value to your business.

In fact, as an entrepreneurial advisor, maximizing your business's value in order to create equity is something you always want to keep your eye on and is the subject we'll turn to next.

CHAPTER 9

Build Maximum Equity

Build Maximum Equity

Throughout this book we've asked you to think like an entrepreneur and to treat your practice as a business. This will enable you to build a simple and elegant business that is a joy to run and that delights your clients. By consistently focusing on building maximum equity, you'll also create an extremely valuable business.

We've saved this seventh strategy—build maximum equity in your business—for the end because we wanted you to first understand how to create a great business that would not only serve fewer, wealthier clients, but would give you the lifestyle you want. (Remember when we urged you to read straight through the book before trying to apply anything? This is the point we wanted you to get to.) Now that you know how to build a great business, we want you to keep your eye on one more thing: building your business to ensure its maximum value.

It may surprise you to learn that the "CEG" in "CEG Worldwide" stands for "Creating Equity Group." As an organization, we embrace equity creation as part of our mission because we've seen far too many advisors at the ends of their careers who have not achieved their dreams. Consider how you were recruited into the industry. Recruiters tell prospective advisors that their greatest challenge will be to decide just how much money they want to make and how soon. With just a little hard work, they say, you'll be able to achieve the American dream. Unfortunately, many advisors have realized only one part of that dream—the hard work.

Think about why you got into the business in the first place. Part of the motivation for many of us was to help solve clients' financial challenges. Having a positive impact on a significant number of successful families is a real accomplishment to be proud of. But while a client-centered focus is important, you must also build your business to support the quality of life you want for your own family as well—if you're not able to take care of your family, then you probably won't be able to do a good job for your clients.

Your clients feel the same way. They want to work with someone who has the self-respect and wisdom to keep his or her own financial house in order. They know that you can't take care of them if you can't even take care of yourself.

So making sure your financial stake in your business is as great as possible makes sense from all perspectives. Your challenge is to focus on building a practice that the marketplace will highly value.

It's never too early to take the steps necessary to build substantial equity in your business. This is true whether you're a sole practitioner or work smack-dab in the middle of a major firm. In fact, as with investing for retirement, the sooner you start making an ongoing investment in equity creation, the better your position will be later on when it comes time to sell or otherwise transition out of your business.

Benefits for Everyone

Thinking like an entrepreneur in order to build a valuable business is both farsighted and completely appropriate regardless of where you happen to work. It doesn't matter if you are employed by a wirehouse, are an independent broker-dealer representative inside a large office or are a registered investment advisor with your own firm. Regardless of your specific situation, building equity will pay huge dividends.

By staying focused on building equity, you will personally be better off, both now and in the long run. Think about the last time you sold a home. In order to make it show well, you very likely spruced it up and made all those minor repairs you'd been putting off. As a result, it never looked or felt better. Similarly, even if you aren't looking to exit your business any time soon, really "taking care of business" now will markedly increase both your cash flow and your enjoyment of your business.

Similarly, as we've shown throughout this book, your clients will be better off because they'll get the attention and world-class service that they want and expect. So a big part of creating a business that is as valuable as possible comes from providing the very consultative client relationship management process and top-notch service that most satisfies your wealthy clients. This puts you and your clients in the same boat, being lifted by the same entrepreneurial tide. The result is a "no-brainer," a win-win for everyone. This makes our first and last strategies—attract wealthy clients and build maximum equity—a mirror image of one another: The very things you do to attract and then retain wealthy clients are also the things that will build tremendous value.

Finally, whether you are in a position to actually sell your business or work in a firm where you can take advantage of increasingly attractive sunset provisions, everyone comes out a winner. When you sell your business to another advisor or firm, clearly they see the value in it and are happy to take over, for a reasonable price that benefits you both, what you've created. And in fact, in recent years we've seen an active and growing marketplace as advisory businesses have evolved and some of the individuals running them have reached traditional retirement age.

If you are employed by a wirehouse, the equation changes slightly, but everyone involved nonetheless will end up benefiting from your entrepreneurial equity-maximizing approach. Because today's firms realize the importance of succession planning and the advantages of incenting their advisors to create as much value as possible, almost all firms now offer sunset provisions that will enable you to tiptoe out of the business over three to five years. And note that while independent advisors have more flexibility in selling their businesses outright, wirehouse advisors have two competitive advantages. They can leverage their firms' brands, and they have guaranteed "buyers" standing by who are ready to finance the transactions.

A typical sunset provision will give you in excess of two times revenue over three to five years, and you'll know the check on the back end is as good as your relationships are now with your existing clients. If you've built a valuable business and your clients stay on with the successor advisor, you'll do very well. If your successor advisor can grow the business even more, you'll do even better. But it all begins with the foundation you leave and the real value that you've built up in your business over time. Obviously, the firms themselves also benefit when advisors follow a value-driven entrepreneurial approach, because such advisors create a much more valuable set of client relationships and business processes that remain for the long term.

The Four Cs of Creating Equity

You can tell whether you're on the road to maximizing the value of your business by objectively assessing the four C's of creating equity. These are the four primary drivers of value in a financial advisory business that will cause buyers (or successor advisors in a big firm) to covet what you've created:

1. Cash flow
2. Clients
3. Company
4. Competitors

1. Cash Flow

The single most important thing you can do to create equity is to maximize your cash flow and profit margins. Every buyer of a business (and every advisor who "buys" a business through a sunset provision transition) takes into account the discounted value of current cash flow. The more cash flow you have, and especially the more your cash flow is growing and the higher your profit margins, the more value you will have demonstrated. In the best of all worlds, your cash flow will continue to grow and your margins will continue to expand in a straight upward-sloping line. An up-and-down or bumpy line is clearly less desirable.

As you consider cash flow, don't mistake it for good revenues. While obviously you can't have a lot of cash flow and good margins without great revenues, cash flow is still the byproduct of good margins. Revenues, on the other hand, are the byproduct of good growth. Financial advisory businesses can generate substantial profit margins at every size, so make sure that you're matching up your costs with your revenues from the get-go.

2. Clients

You want your clients to have a demonstrable pattern of high retention and high satisfaction, a strong tendency to make referrals and a predisposition to not be tied to a single person at your firm (even you). Smart potential buyers will spend a good deal of time looking at your clients. To the extent that your clients all enjoy the same simple and elegant experience of your consultative process, it will be easier for you to demonstrate a high level of satisfaction and ongoing loyalty through a formal process, such as a client survey.

3. Company

You should be able to show high retention and satisfaction of employees or team members, both in terms of their work environment and their compensation. Be prepared to tell success stories of employees or team members who have moved up through the ranks, taken on additional responsibility and grown their compensation along the way.

You also need to be able to demonstrate good business management in these areas:

- Financial management and processes
- Client management and processes
- Employee (or team) management and processes
- Operations management and processes

4. Competitors

You want a business model that competitors either cannot figure out or that is difficult to replicate. Your competitors should be in awe of your business model's growth and profitability. However, don't think that this means that you have to have some sort of complicated trade secret that drives your success. In fact, what competitors are most often in awe of is an extremely simple business that works extremely well.

In this book we've laid out the wealth management business model and shown you how to make it work. Incredibly, CEG Worldwide's latest research shows that only 6.6 percent of surveyed advisors with more than $50 million in assets under management are using this model. This gives you every opportunity to differentiate yourself and leave your competitors in awe of the growth and profitability of your business model. If your business is working so well that your competitors either want to join with you or acquire you, you'll know you're on the right track.

Organic vs. Alternative Growth

You can follow one of two approaches to creating value and equity in your business over time. The first is organic growth, or building a great business by serving your clients well over time. Pursuing organic growth has real advantages. You get to keep control over everything, from the direction of your business and the way it's managed to the number and depth of your client relationships.

The other approach, alternative growth, accelerates growth through acquiring, merging with or partnering with another advisory business. Unfortunately, many studies have indicated that the failure rate among mergers is roughly 70 percent, so you'll want to be very careful about taking an alternative approach when the organic methods we recommend are so reliably successful.

Given the nature of how capital works and grows, any advisor worth his or her salt will experience a reasonable amount of organic growth. But by using the wealth management model and the strategies we describe in this book, your organic growth will look a lot like the alternative growth that other advisors can get only by buying or selling a business, which, as we just stated, can be fraught with uncertainty and unexpected difficulties. As a great entrepreneur who pursues organic growth to build a simple and elegant business, you'll probably be a lot happier. (And if you need help implementing our strategies, you can benefit from the mentoring, coaching or consulting we described in the last chapter.)

Certainly, before you pursue any alternative growth strategy, make sure your business is completely in order, with all equity-maximizing systems in place. If you are in a position to sell your business outright, this will provide you with the highest valuation and the best opportunity to prevent a cultural mismatch that could cause failure. In addition, if you're considering a deal of any type, bring in an outside expert who really knows how to maximize the price you get for your business or to minimize what you have to pay for someone else's. Especially in the case of selling your business, you'll probably only do it once in a lifetime, so if ever there were a time to bring in a true professional, this would be it.

Of course, there's already one true professional in the picture: you. And for the benefit of that true professional, we'll now turn to our final chapter, where we'll provide a framework for transforming the vision we've given you in this book into the reality of your everyday experience.

CHAPTER 10

Making It Real

Making It Real

It's remarkable how well you can do for yourself while doing well for others. The impact you can have on your clients by aligning their financial assets to support their most important values and goals is simply tremendous. Collectively, as financial advisors, we really do have an unbelievable opportunity to change the world in positive ways. At the same time, we can get paid very well and also have an outstanding quality of life. That's about as good as it gets.

Is it easy to make this happen? Frankly, no, it's not, especially at first, and even more so if you're trying to do it all on your own. That's why we wrote this book: to present a direct, no-nonsense road map to success. It's also why we provide the coaching programs described later. If your mission is to build a top-tier wealth management business that makes the world a better place for you and your clients, we want to help you.

The Big Picture

Let's take a step back and take a look at the big picture. Our extensive research shows that there are essentially two types of advisors: investment generalists and wealth managers. And despite the fact that wealth managers unquestionably do better for themselves and have a better quality of life, our 2007 study found that the percentage of advisors using the wealth management model has actually declined over the last few years, down to 6.6 percent. (Recall **Exhibit 4.1**.)

What could explain this? Well, as we write this in 2007, times are generally good but with some significant market volatility. The markets have been rising overall, and most advisors simply don't feel enough pressure to take an objective look at their practices or to consider making any real changes. That may be fine for them, but if you've read this far, it's probably not fine for you.

So what do you do next? How can you actually implement our recommendations? What do you need to do to make it all real?

First, we suggest that you commit these four maxims to memory:

1. **Be successful on purpose.** As we've stressed throughout this book, success demands intentional action. When you begin with the end in mind and commit to the necessary hard work and planning, your odds of success rise dramatically.

2. **Think like an entrepreneur.** Whether you're independent or employed by a big firm, you're in business for yourself. This means that to be extremely successful, you have to think like an entrepreneur who has chosen to be in the wealth management business.

3. **Work with fewer, wealthier clients.** If you're determined to be successful on purpose and are thinking like an entrepreneur, your single best course of action is to identify a niche of wealthy individuals and provide them with the world-class service and consultative wealth management that will delight them and motivate them to provide both additional assets and qualified referrals.

4. **Outsource what you can (and should).** If you attempt to build a highly successful wealth management business on your own, you will fail to reach your full potential. Determine where you add the most value—which in most cases will be client relationship management, expert relationship management and business development—and outsource the rest. Don't try to go it on your own.

Second, review the seven strategies we've presented. The overview in Chapter 1 is a good place to start. With the big picture in mind, it will be much easier to create the road map you'll need to navigate from where you are now to where you want to be in the not-too-distant future.

Third, commit to overcoming the knowing-doing gap that we described in Chapter 2. In accordance with the "Outsource what you can" maxim, you may find that you need some help to bridge the knowing-doing gap.

Ironically, when we founded CEG Worldwide, we thought it would be sufficient to provide financial advisors with research and training as to best practices. But having been through the entrepreneurial fire many times ourselves, we should have realized that knowledge alone isn't enough. Most people, including most advisors, need help in implementing what they learn. Whether you choose us or someone else, we believe that working with a qualified coach, mentor or consultant will dramatically accelerate your efforts to build a successful wealth management business.

The Power of Planning

There's little doubt that virtually every financial advisor is in business to succeed, to enjoy a good income, to serve clients well and to have a great lifestyle. But some advisors are extremely successful, while many others are just hanging on. What's the difference between them?

In our experience, it isn't talent—we've known plenty of incredibly smart, talented advisors who never seem to achieve the level of success they deserve. Nor is it opportunity. We've known advisors who were presented with great opportunities that they never managed to turn into real success.

So what's the key? We believe it's being focused and ready for change. The top advisors envision their success, draw up clear plans for getting there and then find effective ways to incorporate the needed changes into their practices.

Our experience with hundreds of elite financial advisors tells us that they consistently take these actions:

- They formulate a vision of what their lives will be like in the next three years.
- They clearly define the goals needed to realize their vision and then commit to achieving them.
- They identify the strategies and tactics they will need to implement to achieve their goals, with particular attention paid to planning for early wins.
- They execute their strategies and tactics so as to realize their goals and make sure to celebrate wins along the way.
- They and their coaches regularly review their goals so they can stay focused on what's important in their lives.
- They hold themselves accountable for breaking through into higher levels of success.

Top financial advisors understand that once they have an intention to succeed, many of their perceived obstacles will disappear. That is, they intentionally position themselves to achieve success. They understand in their bones that the popular cliché "Where there's a will, there's a way" is quite true.

To maximize the probability that you'll succeed, be clear about your intentions for success. Successful people do what unsuccessful people are not willing to do. In today's marketplace, you have a great opportunity for success—again, despite the fact that more and more advisors are calling themselves wealth managers, there are actually fewer true wealth managers today than there were several years ago—but you must be proactive. We strongly recommend that you purposefully design your own future by creating a road map—a plan—of the steps ahead.

Don't put yourself at a disadvantage by failing to develop a plan. Without one, it's easy to become overwhelmed by the challenges you face. But a plan that incorporates the goals that you are passionate about achieving will keep you focused on your priorities and on track until you manifest your vision.

Making It Real

With your vision and goals clearly defined, and with an intelligent and realistic plan set forth, your next—and far more challenging—step is to take the actions that will achieve your goals.

Successful change is a real challenge in part because typically no one else (e.g., staff or team members, or partners or management) reacts well to change except the person who is driving it. When change comes, we all tend to immediately put our hands up and try to figure out how to avoid it. Behaviorists tell us that 80 percent of us are reactive thinkers who will do anything to avoid change. The other 20 percent are creative thinkers, meaning we initially try to avoid the change but then examine and judge whether it's good or bad change. If we think it's a good change, we'll incorporate it into our lives. When creative thinkers believe it's a change for the worse, they'll figure out ways to get around it.

Even with a road map and a serious commitment, you will face substantial challenges. But that's a good thing. To overcome the obstacles that separate winners from losers, you will be called upon to add substantial value. If it were easy to become a world-class wealth manager, everyone would be doing it.

So when you find yourself butting heads or hearts with management or your team members and you just want to quit—don't. If you are clear about the success you want, have put together a workable plan and are willing to do what it takes to succeed, then surely you will.

So commit yourself to the success you want, create a plan to get there and then begin to turn your dreams into reality. The possibilities that we have described in this book are very real and well within your reach. The strategies we've described are the best ones out there. So if that's what you want, get started—right now. We know you can do it and wish you the very best of success. Your clients and future clients are counting on you.

About the Authors

John J. Bowen Jr. CEG Worldwide's founder and CEO, John Bowen has long been known as a leader in the area of adding value to financial services firms. Bowen started his career as an independent broker-dealer representative and then became a fee-based financial advisor. He was ultimately named the CEO of Reinhardt Werba Bowen (RWB), a money management firm that helped other financial advisors raise billions of dollars in assets. In 1998, Bowen became CEO of Assante Capital Management upon the acquisition of RWB by Assante. He left Assante to start CEG Worldwide in 2000 in order to help advisors realize substantial success through the use of CEG Worldwide's business development systems.

He writes a highly acclaimed monthly column for one of the leading financial services trade journals in the United States, *Financial Planning*. He is the author of several books, including *The Prudent Investor's Guide to Beating the Market* and *Creating Equity: How to Build a Hugely Successful Asset Management Business*.

Patricia J. Abram. A senior CEG Worldwide managing principal, Patricia Abram has 27 years of success in the financial services industry, including five years as senior vice president and chief marketing officer of American Skandia, Inc., where she played a key role in the record-setting growth of that company. Prior to joining American Skandia, she was senior vice president and chief marketing officer of Mutual Service Corporation, where she was also a member of the executive committee and the management committee, oversaw all marketing functions, and was responsible for the training and development of the firm's investment professionals.

A prolific writer and frequent public speaker, she has conducted hundreds of presentations nationally and internationally and has made numerous presentations to the Financial Planning Association, Securities Industry Association, Financial Services Institute, NAVA, the Institute of Certified Financial Planners and national wholesaler groups. She writes a regular column for *Research* magazine.

Jonathan Powell. Jonathan Powell, senior managing principal, has hired and coached hundreds of the industry's top financial advisors—in multiple distribution channels—for more than 25 years.

After starting his career as an independent financial planner in the San Francisco Bay area, he went on to spend more than two decades with Citigroup before retiring to pursue his passion for training and coaching. In his lengthy career, Powell has managed branches for Smith Barney and led Citibank's West Coast brokerage business, overseeing 290 financial advisors and 20 managers. While at Citigroup, Powell was a sought-after speaker for national and regional conferences on topics including time management, financial advisor strategies for success and effective recruiting.

Powell's considerable expertise in developing top-performing financial advisors is a great asset to the clients he serves through CEG Worldwide. Working with many of the nation's top brokerages, he enjoys helping advisors transform their professional and personal lives by using CEG Worldwide's research-backed principles.

Breaking Through: Capturing the Opportunity

Now that you've reached the end of **Breaking Through:** *Building a World-Class Wealth Management Business*, you are probably wondering how to put everything you've learned into action.

You already know that there is a big difference between understanding what works and actually implementing tactics and strategies successfully. Knowledge alone is not enough; you must know how to apply it well.

The goal of CEG Worldwide's research-based coaching programs is to bridge the knowing-doing gap while giving financial advisors proven methods for capturing the wealth management opportunity.

We know that helping advisors move upmarket to become more successful takes more than traditional training—it takes the ongoing support of effective coaching.

Our coaching programs offer the best of both worlds: specific steps and real-world tools that enable advisors to grow their businesses, side by side with expert coaching that ensures that advisors put what they learn to work.

Here is a brief overview of the coaching programs we offer:

HOW DO YOU COMPARE TO THE TOP ADVISORS?

Find Out with a Free Assessment

Don't miss out on your free assessment, available now at www.cegworldwide.com. Just answer a short series of questions and we'll provide a report identifying potential gaps in your practice—plus name the actions you can take to break through to your next level of success. See the reverse side of the dust jacket of this book for the unique code that will give you access to the free assessment.

- Breaking Through. Our intensive one-year coaching program is focused on the essential strategies and key tactics required to successfully attract, win, service and retain the private affluent client.

- Cultivating the Affluent. This comprehensive coaching program offers independent financial advisors invaluable tools for building more profitable businesses. This program is designed specifically for independent broker-dealer representatives and registered investment advisors who want to accelerate their business success.

- The CEG Roundtable. This exclusive three-year program for *Breaking Through* and *Cultivating the Affluent* graduates helps advisors to further master all that they've learned, in order to double their net income and double their free time—all through serving their clients well.

- **Practice Management Forums.** During these intensive two-day forums, advisors master vital wealth management tactics and strategies including how to implement the consultative process and how to focus on an affluent clientele.

Whether you work with CEG Worldwide to capture the opportunity we have presented in *Breaking Through* or choose another path, we wish you every success.

John J. Bowen Jr.

Patricia J. Abram

Jonathan Powell

P.S.: If you're interested in participating in any coaching program offered by CEG Worldwide, check with your company representative in charge of training. We work with many financial institutions and could already have at your firm a program in place that has been specifically designed for your firm and is available to you at a subsidized cost.

Learn much more about CEG Worldwide and its people and coaching programs by visiting www.cegworldwide.com.